The Leopard
and the
Sky God

Retold by Mairi Mackinnon

Illustrated by
Ali Lodge

Reading Consultant: Alison Kelly
Roehampton University

This story is about

the Sky God,

the
leopard,

his drum,

the python,

the elephant

and the
tortoise.

3

Long ago, when the world
was new,

the animals
lived in the forest.

High up above lived
the Sky God.

One day, the Sky God
heard a wonderful sound.

He leaned down and
looked through the trees.

There was the leopard,
playing a great big drum.

He played high

and low.

He played *soft*

and **loud!**

"Hello, Leopard," said the
Sky God.

10

"Sorry," said the leopard.
He shook his head.

"I'll be very careful," said the Sky God.

"No," said the leopard.

But the leopard kept his eye on the drum the whole time.

The Sky God walked away.
"What's the matter?"
asked the other animals.

Leopard won't let me play his drum.

"I wish I had that drum,"
the Sky God said.

"I'll talk to Leopard,"
said the python.

He found the leopard,
playing his drum as usual.

"What do you want?"
growled the leopard.

"May I look at your
drum?" asked the python.

"No!" roared the leopard,

and he showed his long
teeth and his sharp claws.
21

The python slithered
away quickly.

"Well?" said the Sky God.
"Sorry," said the python.

22

"I'm not scared," said the elephant. "I'll talk to him."

23

He soon heard the drum.
Where was the leopard?

The elephant looked
around. There he was —
up in a tree.

"May I look at your drum?" asked the elephant.

"Leave me alone!"
roared the leopard.

27

The elephant shook and
shook the tree...

...but he couldn't shake
the leopard out.

"Well?" said the Sky God.
"Sorry," said the elephant.

It's too difficult.

"Let me try,"
said the tortoise.

29

Now in those days the tortoise had no shell, only a little soft body.

The others laughed.
"You'll never do it."

But the tortoise said,
"Wait and see."

She found the leopard
in his tree.

Mr. Leopard!
Mr. Leopard!

"The Sky God doesn't have a drum," said the leopard.

Oh yes he does.

"It's enormous," said
the tortoise. "He can
climb inside it."

The leopard climbed
down from the tree.

He rolled the drum
along the ground and
crawled inside.

Like this?

"Right inside,"
said the tortoise.

38

Then she looked around
and spotted the leopard's
cooking pot.

Quickly, she clapped
the lid over the end of
the drum.

Then she rolled it along
to the Sky God.

The Sky God
was very pleased.

I don't want it
any more. You
can have it.

Then the tortoise said,
"Sky God, can you do
something for me?"

43

She looked at the drum.
"I would like a shell on
my body...

...so that nothing can
hurt me."

"Yes, of course," said the
Sky God.

The Sky God loved his
drum.

And, when the weather
is stormy, you can still
hear him...

The Leopard and the Sky God is a very
old story from the Asante kingdom in
West Africa (now in the country of Ghana).

Series editor
Lesley Sims

Designed by
Catherine-Anne MacKinnon

First published in 2007 by Usborne Publishing Ltd., Usborne House,
83-85 Saffron Hill, London EC1N 8RT, England. www.usborne.com
Copyright © 2007 Usborne Publishing Ltd.

48

Please return to:
Palmstown Church
3151 Ritner Highway
Newville, PA 17241
(717) 776-6511

"Stormie's book feels like a long overdue, much-needed conversation with an old friend...whose voice I can hear saying, "Your life is valuable; you are worth the effort that it takes to adopt a healthful lifestyle." In the rush and crush and noise of my day, this is a voice worth listening to."

AMY GRANT

"An excellent motivational book, highly informative, a great overview of the functions and the needs of the human body. And a must for anyone who wishes to establish a comfortably disciplined routine for mind, body and spirit for the rest of their lives."

DONNA SUMMER

"If you're like me and feel at times that you are drowning in the quicksand of self-improvement plans, I think you'll find *Better Body Management* and its balanced approach to a healthy lifestyle the lifeline you've been looking for."

DEBBY BOONE

"On taking a break from my acting career to raise my children, I also thought I would take a break from diet and exercise. I soon realized there are more benefits to a good health routine than looking good on TV. *Better Body Management* has provided me with a key element in having the energy and endurance to raise three children under the age of three, and my whole family is grateful for what it has taught me about how to relieve stress."

LISA WHELCHEL CAUBLE

Better Body Management

Practical Tips for a Lifetime
of Health and Fitness
from the Author of
Greater Health God's Way

Sparrow Press
Nashville, Tennessee

Published 1993 in Nashville, Tennessee, by Sparrow Press, and distributed in Canada by Christian Marketing Canada, Ltd.

Printed in the United States of America

97 96 95 94 93   5 4 3 2 1

Library of Congress Cataloging-in-Publication Data

Omartian, Stormie.
      Better body management / Stormie Omartian.
         p.   cm.
      Includes bibliographical references.
      ISBN 0-917143-25-6 : $10.95
      1. Nutrition. 2. Exercise. 3. Body weight—Regulation.
      I. Title.
RA784.054 1993
613/2—dc20   93-23876
                                        CIP

Design by Koechel Peterson & Associates

"*Narrow is the gate
and difficult is the way
which leads to life.*"

MATTHEW 7:14 (NKJ)

"*My yoke is easy
and My burden
is light.*"

MATTHEW 11:30 (NKJ)

Contents

Acknowledgements

My special thanks

- to my husband, Michael, my son, Christopher, and my daughter, Amanda, without whom the work of my hands would have little meaning for me.
- to Bill Hearn, who first had the vision for this book and encouraged me to write it.
- to David Hazard, my talented and witty editor, for his patience and kindness.
- to Kathleen Stephens, who, as managing editor, oversaw this book project through to its completion.
- to Janet Hinde, my good friend and secretary, for going cheerfully and tirelessly along with another book deadline.
- to my dear prayer partners, Lisa Whelchel Cauble, Debra Goldstone, Pamela Deuel Hart, Priscilla Navarro, and Roz Thompson, for their deep commitment to support me and the writing of this book in prayer.
- to the American Council on Exercise (ACE), the Aerobics and Fitness Association of American (AFAA) and the American College of Sports Medicine (ACSM) for their diligent research and dedication to getting us all in shape in the safest and most effective way possible. I drew much of my information from the publications and position papers of these highly respected organizations and I trust their reliability and accuracy.

Introduction

One of the deepest desires of my life and the object of my most fervent prayers is to find the key that will free people who struggle in the area of proper care for their bodies. There are millions who do. If you are not one of them, be thankful that you're in a minority and read on to find out how you can help the rest of us.

Most people carry on a battle with food and a struggle with exercise that is agonizing, exhausting, defeating, and a prelude to the most intense feelings of failure. I've seen convicted and confessed killers have less remorse than many people I know who beat themselves up emotionally because they've eaten too many cookies.

When I wrote my first book on body care about ten years ago, called *Greater Health God's Way* (Sparrow Press), I listed seven steps to greater health. Most people had little or no problem with five of them but there were two areas with which they struggled: *exercise* and *food*. For that reason, I am going to concentrate on those two areas in this book.

The road to life is not easy. The Bible says it's narrow and difficult (Matt. 7:14). But we all know that anything worth having often requires a certain amount of effort and self-sacrifice. The Bible also says if we yoke up with God and give our burdens to him, he makes them easy and light (Matt. 11:30). While we have the responsibility to make wise choices, the burden of carrying them out can be borne by a power greater than us. We can have divine wisdom and enablement to be and do all that we desire.

If you're a person who struggles in the area of body care, or are frustrated by the results of your efforts along those lines, I believe I have some exciting information that can help you. I pray that when you read this book you will be motivated by the truth that is in it, and energized by the Holy Spirit of God to implement these practical suggestions and apply them directly to your life. In other words, when you finish this book I want you to be able to stand up and say, *"Yes! This sounds good to me and I believe I can do it!"*

Better *Body* Management

Chapter 1

The Case For Treating Your Body Right

Can you instantly think of a hundred things you'd rather do than exercise? Do the foods you most like to eat seldom fall into the "healthy-and-nutritious" category?

If so, I understand how you feel because I once felt the same way. However, some years ago, I decided to make health and fitness a goal, the same way I make internal, spiritual growth a goal. Sure, I fail now and then. At those times, I feel just like you do when you fail to eat right and to exercise: guilty, disgusted, sickly, weak, sluggish, depressed. But I've made it a lifelong habit to face and then let go of my failures and lapses quickly—to get right back on-track with regular exercise and with healthy eating.

Believe me, you are not hearing this from someone who has been some kind of health-food purist all her life. There was a time when I would eat an *entire* box of chocolates in one sitting. I drank soft drinks—never water. If there were cookies in the house, I didn't rest until I'd consumed them all! Then I'd go on "health binges" that were so strict and confining I couldn't maintain them for long. So I'd

The truth is,

not one of us

can get away

with doing

whatever we

want with our

physical bodies.

Neglect or abuse

will catch up to

every one of us.

give up on the health kick, and live it up big-time with pizza, soft drinks, ice cream and cake.

When it came to exercise, *I wouldn't.* For months at a time I did nothing—and then in a fitness frenzy I'd go full-speed-ahead to exercise and dance classes. You can imagine that I'd become burned-out, sore, sick, exhausted, injured and *discouraged.* By the end of the first week of my "reform" I would talk myself into taking a break. It would take *months* to recover, and by that time I'd lost interest.

It's strange for me to look back on that time—as if looking at an entirely different person. What changed? I learned the truth about proper health maintenance and physical conditioning. I learned all I could about the why and how of better body management.

For example, I studied to become certified as an aerobic instructor with the American Council on Exercise (ACE) and the Aerobics and Fitness Association of America (AFAA), both of which have abundant solid information about proper body care. More importantly, I grew into a deeper relationship with the Source of life, which balanced my thinking. Growing spiritually gave me insight into the right and wise way to care for ourselves. And it helped me see through the gimmicks—quick-fixes that are no more than a flurry of activity to attempt to ward off the results of a lifetime of bad habits.

I do things differently now, because I know more. My reason for writing this book is so that you can know as much. I want you to know how to properly eat, exercise, rest and play so that you can get the maximum blessing and enjoyment out of life.

The first step to better body management is

seeing the greater picture—that fitness and health are more than looking good in designer jeans. Better body management means seizing life and saying, "I don't want to go through each day tired, weak, fuzz-brained, depressed and barely surviving. I want my life to be marked by clarity, accomplishment, a giving spirit, a positive attitude and joyful anticipation. I want to live it to the best of my ability—serving others and enjoying them, as well as caring for myself."

The truth is, not one of us can get away with doing whatever we want with our physical bodies. Neglect or abuse will catch up to every one of us. If we wait until the sudden shock of a doctor's discouraging report, it may be too late to undo years of bad habits. Even if we survive, the heart attack, cancer or stress-related disease takes its toll. But you can adopt healthy habits now to help you avoid life-limiting illnesses and experience more enjoyment and usefulness in life for years to come.

I don't think for a moment that my health and healing is entirely up to me, or that everything that happens in my life depends completely upon what I do. In fact, I believe the opposite. I'm linked up with the Creator who knows what works best for each one of us and who longs to let his power and life flow through you and me. But the fact is, he has given each of us a brain and a will and we are to use both in caring for our bodies. Deciding to take action, then learning the right actions to take and why—these are the foundation stones on which physical fitness is built.

What Exactly Is Physical Fitness?

The American Council on Exercise (ACE), defines physical fitness as an "enhanced capacity that allows for an improved quality of life." In other words, when you are physically fit your body is improving or maintaining health, not deteriorating. Your heart, lungs and blood vessels work the way they were designed to work. You are increasing your muscle strength and endurance, and you are moving toward good flexibility. Your overall body fat is in a safe-level zone, so that you are maintaining a strong, lean body mass. And you are not chronically fatigued. When you are physically fit, you carry a sense of well-being, an attitude of positive expectancy and an exuberance for life. As a result, you are able to face your problems head-on and handle them without feeling overwhelmed. You have a forward-looking attitude as you face the day.

Isn't that what you're looking for?

Why Do We Neglect Our Bodies?

All of us want these benefits of proper body management. Then why do we struggle so? Why do we so quickly lose control of our attempts at proper body care?

Take our relationship with food, for instance. We give in to uncontrollable urges to overeat, we eat the wrong things and we don't exercise. Then we live in guilt, fear and frustration over it. Here are some reasons we neglect and mistreat ourselves, or make wrong choices with regard to exercise and proper nutrition.

Ignorance: We don't understand exactly what's happening in our bodies or what the real benefits are of the things we need to do. *I don't understand why I have to do this, so I guess I'll just forget it.*

Willful neglect: We decide to do things our own way. *I hate doing this and I don't want to do what I don't want to do.*

Lack of vision or motivation: We don't see a future for ourselves or any purpose for our lives. *I know enough about proper body care to know I need to do it, but what difference does it make? My life's not going anywhere. Who cares if I'm fat, thin, healthy or sick?*

Fear of failure: Due to negative reinforcement from past failures, we move away from anything that can make us feel like a failure again. *I know I need to do something, but I have already failed so many times to exercise and eat right, I fear I'll do the same thing again. I'd rather not try if it means I might fail again.*

Losing touch with reality: We think we are above natural laws. *I don't have to do it because I believe I can get away with not doing it.*

Emotional damage from past trauma: Different fears and phobias can take simple food and exercise choices out of the realm of the practical and simple and into one of emotional complexity. *I feel depressed, angry, sad and disappointed about myself and my life today. If I eat these cookies maybe I'll feel good for a few minutes and get some relief from the pain.*

Having expectations that are too high: No matter what I do, my thighs aren't perfect, my stomach isn't flat and I don't look like a fashion model. Why try?

There are more reasons for not taking proper care of our bodies but after you read this book, ignorance will *not* be one of them. This book will give you useful, practical help, and offer you positive motivation for taking care of your body—one of the Creator's best gifts to you. You will need to make changes—but change is easier when we know that it will bring good consequences, and that it will help us achieve the higher purpose for which we were made.

Perhaps one of the most important benefits you will receive from reading *Better Body Management* is this: You will learn how to become free from using food as a salve for damaged emotions. Emotional injuries are like bodily injuries in that we seek to comfort our inner pain, just as we look for bandages and wraps when we have a physical injury. You don't have to apologize or be embarrassed for emotional wounds. You *can* recover from them. Just as you can provide the right conditions for your body to heal, you can also provide the right conditions

Half Off

If you cannot live without a certain food, schedule a time once a week to indulge yourself, but cut in half the size of your portion. For example, if you usually eat four to six cookies, have two or three instead.

Eat without guilt, remorse or anxiety. Chew slowly. Enjoy every bite. And refuse to eat any more than half of your normal snack intake. Your carefulness will add up over the long haul to a significant reduction in your weight. And your new better-body attitude will favorably affect the way you feel.

for your emotions to recover. In my book on the seven steps to emotional health, called *A Step in the Right Direction* (Thomas Nelson, 1991), I defined emotional health as *"having total peace about who you are, what you're doing and where you're going both individually and in relationship to those around you. In other words, inner health means feeling totally at peace with your past, present and future. It's knowing you're in line with God's ultimate purpose for you and being fulfilled in that."* This kind of well-being, which today so many crave, starts by accepting the fact that you are one of God's unique creations and by learning how to face and deal with guilt and self-condemnation. Why do I raise this issue? Because you and I must get out of the failure mode if we are ever to get a proper perspective on body care: *Better body management is a matter of finding out what's right for you, and asking God to help you do it to the best of your ability.*

Above all, I want you to feel good about what's *ahead* for you in life. When you or I lack motivation or vision for our future, it's usually because we don't like ourselves and feel no one else likes us either. When we feel that way, we see no reason to work at anything and that includes proper body care.

Whether you are in need of motivation, or just useful information, I have worked hard to load this book with practical help—and some useful, fun ideas too—to get you started on a better body management program suited to you. And we'll begin with a look at that masterfully designed collection of muscles, cells and interacting systems you live in—your body—and how you can make it work for you.

Chapter 2

The Golden Benefits of Exercise

"'m too old for this," I insisted, after taping my first exercise video at age 43. How could I know that it was only the beginning? I am now in my 50s, and I've just completed my fifth workout video. I'm always sure that each one will be my last....

Recently a friend handed me a newspaper article and said, "Read this, Stormie. It reminds me of you." In my hands was an interview with a 103-year-old grandmother named Geneva McDaniel, who is an *aerobics instructor*. She was in excellent health, taught daily aerobics classes, and she referred to people in their 60s and 70s as *youngsters*.

I couldn't help but admire that marvelous lady. To be active and healthy at any age is a blessing, but to be able to help others find their way to fitness when you're 103 is inspiring. I don't feel so old when I think about her.

The story of Geneva McDaniel raises an important issue: *consistency*. I once thought that after I hit a certain age my need to exercise diminished. In fact, I've found the opposite to be true. The older you are, the less you can get away with, and the more you need proper exercise and a healthy diet. In fact, once we hit our 30s it seems that everything we do in error or neglect shows up *immediately* in (or on) our bodies. And the older we get, the more serious the consequences. Instead of merely watching our hips get too big for our jeans, we face the risk of heart attack, stroke, cancer or osteoporosis.

Yet a bit of prevention is worth tons of cure. How many of us have seen someone suffer from a disease that could have been prevented—if that person had cared properly for their body? None of us wants to leave here prematurely, nor do we want to become infirm or disabled simply because of our own neglect. We don't want to leave our families, friends, husbands, wives and especially children, before our time. We desire to be vital, productive, energetic and giving right up to the end of our days.

Let's face it: It is possible to achieve that kind of life quality, and we can do it if we begin now with a right attitude toward exercise. Regular physical activity minimizes the natural decline in aerobic fitness and overall health. Staying physically active keeps us more youthful and productive.

You don't need complicated or extended workout programs or expensive equipment and clothes to achieve fitness. In fact, we can simplify our concept of a total body workout by recognizing five areas of physical fitness, all of them interacting, that improve even with moderate exercise. It's important to understand each area, so you can better manage your exercise program. You'll be healthier, stronger and less prone to injury or infirmity if you do something to benefit your body in each area. These five areas of physical fitness are: *cardiovascular endurance, muscular endurance, muscular strength, flexibility* and *body composition.*

What Is Cardiovascular Endurance?

Any part of your body that is not used begins to lose strength and will eventually atrophy, or break down. That's why *all* parts of the body need to be exercised in some way. When considering exercise, it's best to focus first on the cardiovascular and respiratory systems. All of us can benefit from keeping our heart and lungs in good shape.

The cardiovascular system is made up of the heart and the blood vessels. Its purpose is to supply needed energy and nutrients to the brain, muscles and nerves. The respiratory system must be able to get enough oxygen into the blood to supply the working muscles and take waste out of the blood to keep it clean. The best way to keep the cardiovascular and respiratory systems in good shape is with aerobic activity.

Why aerobics?

Aerobic means "in the presence of oxygen." *Aerobic exercise* is any activity that makes use of large muscle groups and causes an increased demand for oxygen over an extended period of time. You are *aerobically fit* if you have cardiorespiratory endurance. That means your heart, lungs and circulatory system can function well enough to supply oxygen while you perform certain types of large muscle movement for 20 to 30 minutes without fatigue or discomfort. Different types of aerobic exercise are walking, running, jogging, bicycling, swimming, rowing, cross-country skiing, stair-stepping and aerobic dance or exercise classes.

Aerobic exercise benefits you by enhancing your body's overall ability to function efficiently, improving your quality of life. A *minimum of 20 to 30 minutes* of nonstop aerobic activity *three to four times a week* will strengthen your heart, improve your capacity to breathe and enable you to better withstand physical, mental and emotional stress.

Regular aerobic exercise will:
- improve your muscle tone and strength
- promote greater bone density (especially important after age 50)
- enhance your cardiovascular system
- help your heart pump more blood with less effort
- lower your resting heart rate, which means your heart doesn't have to work as hard
- help your respiratory system more efficiently move air in and out of your body
- help you to decrease body fat and increase lean body mass
- eliminate chronic fatigue and sluggishness
- reduce high blood pressure

Just Desserts

- *Share desserts rather than eat them by yourself.*
- *At a restaurant, order one dessert and enough forks for each person at the table to try a bite-sized sample.*
- *At home, cut that piece of pie in two. Give the other portion to someone else, or freeze it for another day.*
- *For some nutritional benefit, select a dessert made with fruit or fruit juice.*
- *Change the idea that you deserve a dessert after every meal. One dessert a week is plenty.*

- lower cholesterol
- reduce depression

With regular aerobic exercise you will have more energy, look more vibrant and feel better about yourself and life. How does that sound for an investment of only one to three hours a week?

How the heart cleanses

When you begin to work out aerobically, the muscles you exercise demand more oxygen. That oxygen is transported to the muscles by the work of two systems: the respiratory system and the cardiovascular system. *The respiratory system* transmits oxygen into the lungs when we inhale, so it can be absorbed by the blood. It also removes carbon-dioxide waste out of the cells, so it can be released when we exhale. If we do not breathe deeply, as we are required to do during physical exercise, our wonderful, self-cleansing system will not function adequately, nor will we be able to burn fat. *The cardiovascular system* takes the oxygen from the lungs into the blood and delivers it to the working muscles. It then carries the carbon dioxide back to the lungs to be exhaled. This is a cleansing process that happens continuously and needs to happen efficiently and effectively if we are to stay healthy and fit.

The key is *working muscles*. If we merely sit still and breathe deeply we do not pump more oxygen to other parts of our body, nor do we increase our cardiac output and flush the body of poisons. We just get lightheaded, because when more air flows in and out of the lungs than is necessary, carbon dioxide is exhaled too fast, causing hyperventilation and dizziness. Our muscles need to work while we are breathing in order to draw more oxygen into the blood and make those aerobic benefits kick into gear.

Because blood transports oxygen, our heart rate must increase when we exercise to accomplish this. Your *heart rate* is how many times per minute your heart beats. The *stroke volume* is how much blood the heart pumps with each beat. Multiplying your heart rate by your stroke volume gives you your cardiac output. *Cardiac output* is the amount of blood the heart pumps in one minute.

The ultimate goal of aerobic exercise is to increase cardiac output without increasing the heart rate. In other words, if you can get your heart to pump more blood with each stroke, you can increase the cardiac output without increasing the heart rate. The higher your stroke volume and the lower your heart rate, the healthier you will be. Why? Because your heart will not have to work as hard or beat as fast to deliver the blood. Think of it. By working diligently and faithfully three to four times a week for 20 to 60 minutes, your heart won't have to work nearly as hard as it does when you are not exercising. It's a small investment to help you live longer and healthier.

It's important, however, to begin aerobic exercise slowly. If you do not start at an easy level and work up gradually, your heart will not be able to keep up. It takes time for the heart to increase its capacity to pump blood with each stroke. The good news is it does not require a long period of time for your heart to catch up with your aerobic workout. The secret is to start at an easy pace and slowly increase the *length of time* and the *intensity* of the exercise.

Since your heart is so important to your well-being, it's a good idea to understand how it works. Let's take a quick tour through those hidden and unseen channels that network throughout your body.

The heart has four chambers. Two on top (superior), and two on the bottom (inferior). The two top chambers are called the left atrium and right atrium, and the two bottom chambers are called the left ventricle and right ventricle. The heart receives blood into it from the lungs, where it has been charged with oxygen. This oxygenated blood enters the heart's left atrium, goes through the pulmonary vein down into the left ventricle. From there it spreads out to the body through the aorta and the arteries—into the veins and capillaries. It's there in the capillaries that oxygen is exchanged for waste products. The deoxygenated blood goes back through the veins and into a large vessel called the vena cava, which is like the aorta. Again, it enters the heart through the right atrium, down to the right ventricle. Then it begins its rounds again. Sounds exhausting doesn't it?

This amazing process goes on every moment of your life, so it's crucial to keep this system in top running order. The good news is that regular aerobic exercise will help your entire cardiorespiratory system get stronger. The stronger it becomes, the more blood it can send through with every contraction, and the easier it will be for your heart to do its job. It won't have to beat as hard or as frequently.

So, the first and most important benefit of aerobic exercise is to get and maintain a healthy and efficient heart. Just as important is the need for blood vessels that are strong and elastic. Weak, hard blood vessels can become clogged and lead to arteriosclerosis, a thickening and hardening of the arteries. Clogged arteries to the brain can lead to a stroke. Clogged arteries to the heart can result in a heart attack. Regular cardiovascular endurance exercise can minimize the chances of either of those things happening. Aerobic exercise increases the number of capillaries in your body, which means there can be a more efficient exchange of oxygen for waste products. The number of capillaries supplying nutrients and oxygen decreases anywhere in the body where the tissues are not being used.

So you see now why aerobic exercise to increase your cardiovascular endurance is a must for greater health and fitness.

Muscular Endurance and Its Advantages

Along with cardiovascular endurance, we need muscular endurance. This means being able to use our muscles without undue fatigue. Muscular fitness does not mean just strength, it also means *endurance*. Muscular endurance is the length of time or number of times a muscle or muscle group can repeatedly exert force without fatiguing.

Okay, so you're not into bulging biceps or a rippled abdomen. But think in terms of all you need to accomplish in a day, week, month or year. How many times will you go to work, do the laundry, take your children to school, prepare a meal, clean your house, work in the yard? How many times will you be able to repeat this work, and for how long, if you have little muscular endurance?

Muscular endurance is one of the first things we lose as we age, unless we consciously do something to prevent it. The best way to stave off that part of the aging process is with aerobic exercise, because it trains your muscles to work over an extended period of time. By repeating specific movements, muscles improve their capacity to function. Muscles that develop endurance are those that are worked repeatedly over an extended period of time.

When we work specifically on the muscles needed for lifting, or swinging a racquet or golf club, or hoeing and raking, or dancing, we can expect longer use of those muscles—and more grace, flexibility and stamina. *What benefits!*

In order to develop endurance, do a range of aerobic exercises at least three times a week, for 20 to 30 minutes. That should be your *goal*, not necessarily what you do the first week. Begin with an amount of time you can handle, and work up from there. If you're just starting out as a fast walker or with an aerobic workout tape and you find you can only go for five minutes, don't get discouraged. Be thankful you can do that much—and keep focused on higher goals. In your next workout, try to go six minutes. Then increase your workout a minute every week. If you stop exercising for a week or

Although the days of having to kill ourselves with exercise are over, we still need to extend our endurance a little each time we work out.

25

more, go back and start again where it is comfortable.

I want to point out something: It's true that the days of having to kill ourselves with exercise are over, but we still need to extend our endurance a little each time we work out. When we do, we increase our chances for health and well-being as we get older.

It isn't necessary to push ourselves to exhaustion with any workout. On the contrary, pushing ourselves too hard puts us at risk of injury, fatigue, discomfort and discouragement—and we lose the benefits of aerobic exercise. But if there is not a demand for improvement, our bodies will not respond.

Sometimes the older we get the harder it is to increase our endurance above a certain level. If that's true for you, find the level that you can comfortably maintain, and then create a plan—including a combination of exercise routines and sports, if you like—to help you maintain that endurance. For example, if you feel you can never go beyond a 20-minute aerobic workout, then make it as much fun as possible to keep yourself at that level. Sometimes just maintaining in life is effort enough.

Be forewarned: if you stop regular exercise, your cardiovascular system and other organs and muscles *will* revert to the lower level of functioning they had before you started. No, this doesn't mean that if you stop exercising for a week you'll lose everything you've done. It just means that you can only sustain long-term benefits by taking a reasoned, well-planned, consistent approach to exercise that will benefit you your whole life. And that is far better than making a once-a-year discovery that your slacks don't fit, then responding with a frenzy of dieting and working out. The point is to change your focus and mindset, so that you consistently care for that great gift—your body.

How To Develop Muscular Strength

Besides cardiovascular endurance and muscular endurance we also need *muscular strength*. Strong muscles allow us to work and play without being injured in the process. Muscular endurance exercises will not necessarily improve strength, but exercise that improves strength will improve endurance. Muscle strength is the force or power that a muscle or muscle group can exert during contraction.

After age 30, there is a decrease in the actual number and size of our muscle fibers, and therefore a decline in our muscle mass. Because the size of a muscle is directly related to its strength, our strength deteriorates along with the muscle fibers. We can stop this deterioration and improve our strength by increasing our muscle mass.

Don't throw up your hands and say, "That's it! I don't even have time for 30 minutes of aerobics to develop cardiovascular and muscular endurance—let alone a weight-lifting program to increase muscle mass. Count me out." It may sound overwhelming now, but you'll be surprised at how much lean body mass you can build in a very short time. If you lifted weights 10 minutes a day, three days a week, you would see such a difference in your muscle strength and definition that you would probably increase your efforts to 20 minutes a day—without me badgering you. Fit these few minutes in right after your aerobic workout, or on the days in between your aerobic exercises.

Here is the best news: Muscular strength builds lean body mass—and lean body mass burns calories, even when you're not doing any physical activity. Having a good proportion of lean body mass will help you maintain better body fat control. (I find that *very* motivating!)

Getting a grip

When I joined a new health club a few years ago, I had the complete battery of fitness tests: a cardiorespiratory endurance test using a bicycle ergometer, a three-minute step test, a timed bent-knee sit-up test, a push-up test, a sit-and-reach flexibility test, and a skinfold test. I passed these tests with flying colors, and was at the top of the chart in all fitness levels…then came the test for upper body strength.

I failed that one completely. I was on the lowest edge of the chart.

According to the results of that test, I didn't have a bicep, tricep, trapezius or a latissimus dorsi muscle that was even *close* to doing its job. I knew why, but I didn't know what to do about it. Because of a serious dislocated-shoulder injury when I was about seven, I had always tried to protect my shoulders from injury. Every time I lifted something that was too heavy or I lifted it the wrong way, my shoulder would go out and I would experience the most excruciating pain. I

Environmentally~ Induced Energy Depletion

Too much noise, irritating lights, cramped space, confusing clutter, poor air quality—all contribute to nervous tension, restlessness, frustration, anxiety and stress.

Stop, look and listen—and determine if you are being drained by environmental stressors. Your immune system might be working overtime in response to your environment. You need fresh air, a good light source and non-stress conditions in which to live and work. This is not a luxury.

resolved to never risk that, if at all possible. As a result, I didn't lift *anything* and ended up with the weakest upper body muscles that my young, personal trainer-examiner had ever seen in his short life.

He immediately put me on an exercise program with ultra-sophisticated machines, and also a program I could do at home with two-pound weights. According to all I have read and experienced since, he was on-target with his prescription. In a matter of weeks, working three times a week for just 10 to 15 minutes, I began to see muscles appear. Instead of bones with flab on them, I developed arms that had strength and shape. I noticed that I could pick up a large pot of spaghetti sauce without dislocating my wrist. (I had done that once.) I could manage my own carry-on luggage without injuring my shoulders and back. (I had done that more times than I could remember.) I found that as long as I worked out with weights, I didn't have any of the problems I used to have.

You, too, can develop strength where you thought you had none. It's not hard, it doesn't take much time and it works. All you need are two small hand weights. Start with something under five pounds, or whatever you can lift five times in a row without straining yourself. (Check out the instructions on *"Working Out With Weights, page 51."*) Just wait till you see the benefits.

Learning To Be Flexible

Flexibility is the fourth aspect of physical fitness and, unfortunately, it is not as highly valued as it should be. Having rigidity and stiffness in *any* part of our lives—whether spirit or body—is a sign of aging. When we are inflexible, we become limited and unbalanced in our movements, which can lead to injury. When people fall, it is often because they have poor balance and body control. They don't have the strength and flexibility needed in their muscles to control movement and stay balanced.

The older we get, the less flexible we become. That's because we tend not to be as active, our circulation is not as good and the collagen fiber in our body breaks down. The effects of all this can be slowed, however, if we include some stretching in our exercise program.

Flexibility is determined by the range of motion possible around a joint. It is limited by age, joint structure and ligaments, none of which can be altered. The only way to increase flexibility is to gently stretch muscles and tendons that control joint movement. That's why every time we do aerobic exercise we need to include some kind of stretching and flexibility-enhancing exercises as well.

The perfect time to stretch is at the end of your aerobic exercise, when your body is warmed up. It's the time when you're least likely to injure yourself and most likely to make the greatest difference. There must always be a cool-down period after aerobics, and stretching can be part of that cool-down. Stretching exercises can also be included in the calisthenic section of your workout, when you're working specific muscles like abdominals, legs, buttocks and inner thighs. It's important to stretch the muscles you have just worked in order to prevent soreness or stiffness.

Static Stretching vs. Ballistic Stretching

The two distinctive types of stretching are *static* stretching and *ballistic* stretching. Static stretching is the only kind you will want to do.

Let me explain why.

Ballistic stretching is the rapid, high-force, short-duration bouncing movements that we have all experienced. This impact actually works against the result we want. When a stretch is too sudden or jarring, there is also a sudden contraction in response, which increases muscle tension instead of relaxing it. This is our body's natural protective measure to prevent injury.

Static stretching, on the other hand, means holding a steady position with muscles at their greatest length, while still being comfortable. The static stretch should be held for at least 10 to 30 seconds to get the full benefit. That means it is done slowly, gently, with a low amount of force, and for a longer period of time. When you stretch this way, there is little risk of injury and it helps alleviate muscle soreness.

Why does this kind of stretching work best? Because there is a sensory organ within each tendon, where it connects to the muscle, called the *Golgi* tendon organ. This causes the inhibition of the muscle group when it is stimulated. As you slowly relax into a stretch, the *Golgi* tendon organ sends a signal that there is no danger and it allows the muscles to relax instead of contracting to avoid injury. It is this protective mechanism that makes slow stretching safer and protects muscles from injury.

Do not stretch without some kind of warm-up. When your muscles are warm and there is blood in the area due to increased circulation, there will be far less chance of injury. Full stretching should not be done in your warm-up, because the whole idea of a warm-up is to increase muscle temperature. Stretching does not increase muscle temperature. When you wait until your muscles are warm and *then* stretch, you'll see a greater gain in flexibility. It's best to warm up all your muscles by warming up the entire body, as opposed to trying to just warm up the area you want to stretch.

The best and safest way to stretch is to align your body so that you can stretch the long line of the muscle without any twisting. Move into each stretch slowly and easily to stimulate the *Golgi* tendon organ, which relaxes the muscles, and not the stretch reflex, which tightens them. When you get to your full range of motion, hold the position for 10 to 30 seconds. Breathe in deeply and exhale as you relax into the stretch.

Remember to keep your body balanced. Work out, strengthen and stretch opposing muscles. If you have stretched the hamstrings (back of the upper legs), be sure to stretch the quadriceps (front of the upper legs), as well. The body can get out of balance with some muscles tight and others overstretched.

Don't ever try to compete with anyone else when it comes to stretching. Flexibility is entirely an individual thing. Some people are naturally flexible, some are not. I used to see younger women in my exercise classes walk in and throw themselves into a full split before class had even begun, and I'd berate myself for not being able to do that. Eventually, I came to terms with the fact I will never be able to do a full split—and I'm still a fulfilled person. How flexible everyone else is has absolutely nothing to do with you.

Different days also bring different degrees of flexibility for all of us, due to weather, time of day, temperature, your physical condition and stress levels. Also, one side of the body is usually more flexible than the other because it is used more. Don't ever stretch beyond what is comfortable, no matter what you were able to do the day before. You should never experience pain. In fact, stretching should feel *good* to you. If it goes beyond that point of feeling good, STOP. You've gone too far.

Maintaining Balance In Body Composition

The body can be viewed in four major categories: The organs (which includes the skin), the muscles, bones and fat. *Body weight* is divided into two categories: lean body mass and body fat. The lean body mass includes the organs, muscles and bones. This is the active part of the body. Body fat is not active but stores energy for use during exercise. Having the proper balance between lean body mass and fat is very important to your health and fitness.

There are two different types of body fat: essential body fat and excess body fat. Essential body fat is just that—essential to life. The percentage of fat that women need is 8 to 12 percent, and for men it is 3 to 6 percent. We can't live without at least that much. Women need more than men because of our more complex reproductive systems. That's why our reproductive systems will shut down when body-fat levels get too low. Women who suffer from anorexia often stop menstruating, or find they are unable to conceive. That's because when body fat falls below 17 percent, it can trigger a hormone change or alter metabolism to such an extent that it affects the menstrual cycle.

We also must have a certain amount of *storage fat*. Women need 15 to 25 percent. Men need 12 to 15 percent. More or less than that can be a hindrance. Our body composition has to be in proper balance if we are to have optimum health. This is done through proper diet and aerobic exercise. (More about that in Chapter 6, "Controlling Body Fat.")

These are the five areas of physical fitness to consider as you design your own exercise program. The good news is that you don't have to have five separate workouts in order to accommodate all of them. You just need to have one good workout program that includes each one.

This is not difficult, and it can be fit into your busy schedule. So, you don't think this is possible? Let me show you how....

Chapter 3

Creating Your Own Exercise Program

When setting up your own exercise program, choose some type of aerobic exercise you would be *interested* in doing for at least 20 to 30 minutes, three to four times a week. There are many different possibilities that work equally well.

For example, you could join an aerobics class, or work out on an exercise bike, stair-step machine or rowing machine. You could jog, hike, stair-climb or walk fast. Or you could buy an aerobic exercise video. [May I recommend my *Better Body Workout Video (Sparrow, 1993)?*] If you are athletic, you could skate, swim, jump rope or cross-country ski.

If performed at the same intensity, duration and frequency, one form of aerobic exercise is as good as another. Because there is little difference between them as far as aerobic improvement, pick an activity you enjoy. Or better yet, choose a variety of activities.

The idea is to select activities that use large muscle groups, and can be done rhythmically and maintained continuously. It must be a *lower intensity* activity that can be maintained over a longer period of time, as opposed to a *high intensity* activity that can only be done for a short period of time.

I prefer going to a good gym that has great instructors. I find it invigorating and challenging because I try harder in a class situation, and out of respect for the teacher I am less likely to cut the workout short. I can't always find the time to do that though. Fortunately, I enjoy working out on the stair-step machine, providing I have something good to read, listen to or watch to make the time fly. Because I don't have the opportunity to read or listen to tapes as often as I would like, doing either of those while exercising is a great incentive for me.

Whatever activity you choose, make it something you can do regularly without dread. It doesn't have to be miserable and burdensome. This is a time for you to enjoy.

Before You Do Anything...

The shape of things

Before you start any exercise program, know what kind of shape you're in. If you are under 30, you should have had a medical check-up in the last year. If you are between 30 and 34, you should have had an exam, including an EKG, within the last three months. If you are over 35, you should have had a physical examination within the last three months that includes an EKG *plus* a stress test. No matter what your condition, ask your doctor for advice when beginning an exercise program. A check-up will reveal if there is any medical condition, such as heart disease, high blood pressure, arthritis or anemia, that could limit the results you want or require a special individualized program by a qualified professional.

Health clubs often require written clearance from your doctor before you exercise if any of the following risk factors are present: you are a man over age 40 or a woman over age 45; you've been pregnant or had surgery of any kind within the last three months; you've had heart disease, high blood pressure, chronic bronchitis, emphysema, asthma, diabetes mellitus or other chronic illness; you've had any back, muscle or joint problems; or you've had problems exercising in the past.

You need to know that you are at risk for heart disease if you have any of the following risk factors: you are a smoker; you are more than

20 percent over your ideal weight; there is a history of heart problems in your mother, father, sister or brother; you have high cholesterol; you have high blood pressure; you are under long-term high emotional stress; you are a man over 65; you are physically inactive; or you have diabetes. If you have any of these risk factors you must ask your doctor for medical clearance, even if you are just going to be exercising in your own home.

Proper shoes

Another thing you need *before* you exercise is appropriate shoes for the activity you've chosen. Proper-fitting, good supportive athletic shoes are the most important and possibly the only piece of equipment you need. Don't attempt to do any form of exercise without them, except of course that which can't be done as well with them, such as swimming. Good shoes absorb shock, support arches and protect feet from injury.

Be sure to choose your shoes carefully. Don't make hasty decisions, or opt for the cheapest shoe available. Buying the wrong shoes can lead to injury and misery, to the extent that you lose interest in exercising. When trying on shoes, jog in place, both on your toes and flat-footed, to see how they feel. Your toes should not touch the end of the shoe and you

Take a Vacation From Negative Attitudes

Make a short list of negative attitudes you have, and take a three-day break from them.

If you're a critical or depressed person, for example, decide that for three days you will deliberately find the positive side to every issue, situation or person. You'll be amazed how much better you digest your food, how rested you feel...and how much more energy you have at the end of the week!

shouldn't feel any pain or pressure points. The shoes must be flexible at the ball of the foot and the sole should be wide enough to provide stability. Your foot should not slip around inside the shoe. The heel should be held in place and the ankle stable, yet you should be able to wiggle your toes. You should feel secure in your shoes, and know that you have stability and good support.

Your shoes should provide adequate support for your inside long arch, because this part of the foot absorbs much of the shock. The metatarsal arch also should be supported adequately. Good inserts are available at athletic shoe stores, but if possible, check with a podiatrist specializing in sports medicine before adding them to your exercise shoes. High-top shoes give extra support to the ankle, but don't depend on them to prevent sprained ankles.

Don't go for the shoe that is the hot style at the moment. Rather, look for the shoe that feels secure, stable and comfortably supportive at all times during movement.

Don't eat before exercising.

Plan workouts so that you don't eat for at least one to two hours before exercising. Why? Because when you exercise, blood goes to the working muscles and away from the intestines where food is being digested. Food will not be processed properly if you exercise too soon after eating. It is best to eat *carbohydrates* before exercising, because they take around three hours to digest as compared with protein, which takes twenty-four hours. Often, people don't follow this guideline and become discouraged because they are sluggish, fatigued, slightly nauseated or heavy feeling when they exercise. Following this guideline can make all the difference in your success.

Always Begin With A Proper Warm-up

Before you do any kind of exercise, be sure to warm up for five to ten minutes. That will increase the oxygen and blood flow to the working muscles and warm up the muscles by increasing your core body temperature, thus reducing the risk of injury. A proper warm-up also helps you avoid a build-up of lactic acid, so that you can work longer without having to stop. It also decreases the chances of having an abnormal heart beat *(cardiac arrhythmia)*. A warm-up increases flexibility of the muscles, tendons and ligaments, and prepares the body for more vigorous exercise that is to come. This allows you to have a full range of motion without having an injury, as well. Because the warm-up prepares the body for the demands that will be placed upon it, use movements that specifically prepare you for the aerobic movements you will be doing.

Correct body alignment.

It's important to keep your body in proper alignment at all times— *but especially when you are exercising.* This keeps you from injuring yourself, and it insures that you will get the best results for the effort you put out. Start your workout with that in mind. Fortunately, you will be working slowly in the beginning, so pay extra attention then to correct body alignment.

What is correct body alignment? To begin with, the abdominal muscles must always be held in firmly. It helps me to think of it as trying to get your navel to touch your backbone. You can't really do that, of course, but attempting to do so correctly pulls in the abdominal muscles. No matter what exercises you are doing, keeping the abdominals in protects the back and strengthens and tightens the abdominal muscles as well.

Second, your shoulders should be relaxed—back and down, not up or forward. I've found that the best way to accomplish this is to lift the sternum out. The sternum can be found by locating the point where your ribs meet in front and then moving up about two inches between the breasts. Pushing out the sternum takes pressure off the neck, shoulders and jaw, and the shoulders automatically go back.

Third, body weight must be balanced over the entire foot, not bending forward or leaning back. The pelvis should rest over the hip joints and not tilt forward, giving you a curved back, or backward, giving you a swayback. Curving in either direction puts strain on the back. If the pelvis tilts forward, the likely cause is weak abdominal muscles. If it tilts back, it's probably the result of weak lower back and hip muscles. The knees should not be hyperextended, because this puts pressure on

Just a Little Bit of Fruit Juice Makes the Water Go Down

If you do not enjoy drinking plain water, try making it palatable by adding a little fruit juice. Try juice from half a fresh lemon, lime or orange squeezed into a 16 oz. glass of water. Other good choices are one-fourth cup of cranberry, blackberry or apple juice. This simple addition can make it easier for your body to get adequate hydration.

the lower back, resulting in back pain.

A great beginning

When you start your warm-up, keep the range of motion and intensity level low until the body is properly warmed up. Start with isolated muscle warm-up exercises, and be sure to warm up all the muscles that you'll be using.

Work the muscles and joints slowly, gently and with great control. Start from the top of the body and work down, or from the feet and work up. For example, start warming up the neck, then the shoulders, upper back, arms, chest, rib cage, waist, lower back, continuing with the inner thigh, quadriceps, hamstrings, calf, ankles and feet. No matter which order you go in, make sure you do some warm-up exercise for each one of these areas. Isolate each muscle, and have it gently do what it's supposed to do, making sure that it is done with proper body alignment and without any stress or strain.

Then progress to movements that use large muscle groups, so the core temperature of the body begins to rise. This will raise your heart rate and increase cardiac output, oxygen intake and coordination. The large muscle movements are similar to what you will do in an aerobics class, only the movements are not as broad. They are still slow and simple. Remember, the purpose is to warm the body *and* prevent injury. All it takes is one little muscle pull to put you out of commission for a couple of weeks and you can lose momentum and interest in exercise entirely.

Near the end of the warm-up, stretch the muscles you will be using in the aerobics section—for example, the calf muscles or the leg muscles (hamstrings and quadriceps). This is not the kind of stretching that increases flexibility. That will come at the cool-down at the end. This stretching limbers the body enough to prevent injury. Because stretching will not warm up the body, the best time to stretch is the *end* of the warm-up.

In the past, I often came to aerobics class late and missed the warm-up—not knowing how crucial it is, or how far-reaching the benefits. I no longer do that. I realize now that the only injuries I've had while exercising came when I did not properly warm up and forced a muscle to do something it was capable of, but not ready to do. When you stretch, make sure all stretches are static—long, slow and sustained for 10 to 30 seconds. Once your body is thoroughly warmed up, you can move on to the aerobic workout.

What Happens When We Do Aerobics

When we exercise aerobically, our need for oxygen in the working muscles increases. The body responds to this need by increasing the heart rate and pumping more blood each beat (increased stroke volume) in order to deliver more oxygenated blood. The lungs take in more oxygen in order to get it into the blood, and the blood cells release carbon dioxide as waste products.

It takes about two to four minutes for the body to meet these metabolic demands for more oxygen. That's why it's important to start slowly and work up gradually to peak speed. When you do, you will reach what is called *steady state*, when the delivery and utilization of oxygen is meeting the metabolic demands. At that point you feel you could go on indefinitely. If you never reach that state, chances are you started out too intensely, leaving you winded, exhausted and unable to continue for long. Give your body time for the supply of oxygen to catch up with the demand. To avoid problems, breathe slowly and deeply, inhaling through the nose and exhaling through the nose or mouth.

Don't hold your breath!

Don't ever hold your breath while exercising—especially during aerobics. When you do, it hinders the return of blood to the heart, which in turn reduces the stroke volume (amount of blood pumped in one beat). Remember, the higher the stroke volume, the lower the heart rate and the more efficient the delivery of blood. The blood in our body is distributed according to need. When we are resting, the brain, heart, lungs, liver and kidneys get most of it. When we exercise, blood flows to the muscles to produce ATP (adenosine triphosphate) for energy and to the skin to dissipate body heat. When we hold our breath, none of the above can happen efficiently.

As the muscles need more oxygen during exercise, cardiac output increases to deliver that oxygen. Endurance is your cardiovascular system's ability to deliver oxygen and dissipate internal body heat. You condition the cardiovascular system when you create an increased demand for oxygen over an extended period of time through aerobic exercise. Holding your breath can slow down the development of endurance.

How much time do I need?

According to the American College of Sports Medicine, your aerobics workout can be anywhere from 15 to 60 minutes long, depending on your level of fitness. Twenty to 30 minutes of aerobics works well to provide the cardiovascular conditioning and to burn enough calories to balance your body composition.

If you only have a half-hour to work out, try this:
- 5 minute warm-up
- 20 minutes of aerobics
- 5 minutes of cool-down and stretching

If you have 45 minutes to exercise, try this:
- 5 minute warm-up
- 20 minutes of aerobics
- 5 minutes of aerobic cool-down
- 10 minutes of body sculpting exercises for abdominals, buttocks and thighs
- 5 minutes of slow stretching

If you have 60 minutes, try this:
- 8 minutes of warm-up
- 30 minutes of aerobics
- 7 minutes of aerobic cool-down
- 15 minutes of calisthenics for abdominals, buttocks and thighs
- 5 minutes of slow stretching

Times can be adjusted to suit your needs. Just make sure you never have less than a five-minute warm-up and a five-minute cool-down. If you intend to do an aerobic section longer than 20 minutes, increase the warm-up/cool-down times as well.

Finding Your Target Heart Rate

As I mentioned earlier, the purpose of the aerobic section is to improve cardiovascular endurance. Make sure you are doing this by keeping your heart rate at a certain level for a specific amount of time.

The easiest method of determining what that level should be is the maximal heart-rate formula. It requires the simplest mathematics skills. (If you're like me, you avoid complicated mathematical calculations.) I've found this method to be easy—I wouldn't be doing it if it weren't! *Please don't skip this section. If you are going to do aerobics, you need to know this.*

The target heart-rate zone consists of two numbers—the upper and lower limits for your heart rate. Keeping your heart rate between these two numbers allows you to see benefits from your exercise while not harming yourself. The safest exercising heart rate is 60 to 80 percent of your maximum heart rate. (A beginner who is out of shape might want to start at 50 percent, then work up.) Working below 60 percent won't give you the results or improvement you want. Working above 80 percent puts you at risk of injury.

I'll take you through a step-by-step process of finding your target heart-rate zone. Calculate it once every year, after your birthday, because the results are related to your age.

Follow these simple steps:

Step 1: *Subtract your age from 220.* The number 220 is considered the maximum heart rate for infants. Every year of our lives, our heart rate goes down by approximately one beat. I'll do my age as an example and you do the same with *your* age.

	My Age	*Your Age*
Maximum heart rate:	220	220
Minus your age:	- 50	-___
Maximum heart rate for your age:	170	

Step 2: *Take the maximum heart rate for your age and multiply it by 60 percent to find the low end of the target heart-rate zone.*

	My Age	*Your Age*
Maximum heart rate for your age:	170	___
Multiply by 60 percent:	x.60	x.60
Low end of target heart-rate zone:	102.00	

Step 3: *Take the maximum heart rate for your age and multiply it by 80 percent to find the high end of the target heart-rate zone.*

	My Age	*Your Age*
Maximum heart rate for your age:	170	___
Multiply by 80 percent:	x.80	x.80
High end of target heart-rate zone:	136.00	

My target heart-rate zone is *102–136.* What is *yours?*

When working out, determine whether you are working in your target heart-rate zone by taking your pulse for 10 seconds and then multiplying the number of heartbeats by 6. This will give you the number of times your heart beats per minute.

The last time I exercised, I took my pulse for ten seconds and I counted twenty-one beats. I multiplied it by 6, which came out to be 126—right in the middle of my 102–136 target heart rate zone. That means I am working hard enough to make a difference, but not hard enough to hurt myself. A number lower than the low end of your target heart rate zone indicates you need to work a little harder. A number higher than your high-end heart rate, means you need to slow your pace. Do not stop suddenly, but rather slow down gradually.

Once you get used to working within your target heart-rate zone, you won't have to take your pulse every time you exercise. As long as you are doing the same type of exercise you'll be able to tell whether you're working in the target heart-rate zone or not. You should always breathe comfortably and be able to carry on a conversation while exercising. If you become too winded to talk, decrease your exercise intensity. When you change the type of aerobic exercise you are doing, or if you take off more than a week, check your heart rate again. Always work at a pace that is compatible with your fitness level.

Pulse sites

There are a number of places on your body to take your pulse, but the best place is on the wrist, called the *radial pulse site.* To take your pulse, place the index and middle fingers (not the thumb) of your right hand on your left wrist, just down from the left thumb and below the wrist bone. Rotate the left hand so the palm faces up; the fingers of your right hand should feel a soft indentation. Press down lightly and move your fingers around slightly until you feel a good strong pulse. Even if you have trouble feeling a pulse now, you'll be able to clearly detect one after you start exercising.

You can also take your pulse in the neck, the *carotid pulse site,* by placing the index and middle index fingers to the side of the throat, straight down from the outer corner of the eye. This is not my favorite pulse site because if my heart rate is elevated and I press too hard at this site it can interrupt blood flow and slow the heart. Never press on both sides of the neck at once.

The best time to check your heart rate is five minutes after beginning

Listen at

all times to

what your

heart, brain,

lungs, muscles,

ligaments and

tendons are

telling you

about your level

of training;

don't try to

keep up with

anyone else.

the most active part of your aerobics. It's good to do it again just before the aerobic cool-down. During the first three minutes of aerobics you are not yet working aerobically, so it makes no sense to take your pulse then. If you feel you have overworked, you can take it again after the final cool-down stretch. If your heart rate has not gone down to below 60 percent at that time, you need to continue the cool-down. It's important to keep moving (walking slowly will work) while you are taking your pulse.

The Aerobic Workout

At least 20 minutes of aerobic exercise, done within your target heart-rate zone, burns calories and improves cardiovascular endurance. Working 30 minutes at a lower intensity is better. If you can only exercise five to 10 minutes in the beginning, that's fine. But try to increase the time by a minute or more with each workout. Within a month, you should be able to do 20 minutes of low-impact aerobics. If you can't work out for 20 minutes by that time, you may be working too hard. Work at an easier pace so you can go longer. Only those who are very fit should work at the upper end of their heart rate. Going above that limit will put you at risk of injury.

Even if you've done a thorough and complete warm-up, you must still move slowly into the aerobic section. This allows your cardiovascular and respiratory systems enough time to take in adequate oxygen and get your heart rate up to where you want it to be for most of the workout. The difference between the warm-up and this slow and easy beginning is that it involves continuous large-muscle movements and none of the smaller-muscle isolations of the warm-up.

No matter what you've chosen for your aerobics workout—high-impact or low-impact aerobics, stair-stepping, cycling, jogging, fast walking—individualize your workout to benefit you. Listen at all times to what your heart, brain, lungs, muscles, ligaments and tendons are telling you about your level of training; don't try to keep up with anyone else. Are you breathing too hard? Are you dizzy? Are you in any pain? Do you feel tightness anywhere on your body? Do you feel nauseated or light-headed? Are you too winded to carry on a conversation? If the answer to any of these questions is yes, gradually bring yourself to a stop.

Stopping gradually involves decreasing your intensity by applying less force with each movement, adjusting your range of motion by taking smaller steps and using smaller arm movements. If you feel you're not working hard enough, do the opposite and increase your heart rate by applying greater force to each movement, taking bigger steps and using larger arm movements.

If you are doing high-impact or low-impact aerobics, be sure the floor you're working on is resilient. You are asking for problems by performing high-impact running, jumping or jogging on cement. Conversely, exercising on thick carpeting can make the foot unstable, and may cause you to twist an ankle. The best floor for exercise is wood suspended on an air cushion (good exercise studios and health clubs have them) or a thin carpet. Be aware if you are putting too much strain on your body by stressful jarring. Remember not to walk or jog on your toes. Your heel should come down to the floor also.

As you gradually increase your intensity, you will get to the place called *steady state*, a level you can maintain for a period of time. At that point, your heart, lungs and cardiovascular system deliver oxygen to every part of the body, and you are able to breathe comfortably and steadily. Aerobically fit people can work longer and recover more quickly. If you are not yet fit, don't work as long and allow more time to recover with a longer cool-down time.

If you don't have access to a gym or exercise class, a video machine, exercise video or aerobic exercise equipment, then march in place, go for a fast walk, jog, jump rope or walk up and down stairs for 20 to 30 minutes.

The Aerobic Cool-down

Just as you started slowly and worked up to peak aerobics, you must gradually decrease the same way. When you are ready to stop, take your pulse again. If it is not below your target heart-rate zone, keep walking around until it is.

According to the Aerobics and Fitness Association of America, cardiac problems most often occur not during exercise, but after it is over. If you stop exercising suddenly, the blood circulating in the lower extremities will pool there and be unable to return quickly to the heart and brain. Your blood pressure then drops, causing an irregular heart beat (cardiac arrhythmias). The decreased blood flow to the brain causes dizziness, nausea and, possibly, fainting. So, continue moving your arms and legs, gradually decreasing your exercise intensity, to avoid pooling blood in lower parts of body and to help return the blood as quickly as possible to the heart.

Body Sculpting In Ten Minutes

After your aerobics workout, work on firming and developing specific muscles (without using weights). This part is called calisthenics, muscle strengthening, floor work or body sculpting. These exercises for abdominals, buttocks, hips, thighs, hamstrings and quadriceps are designed to give the muscles shape, definition and tone, and improve their strength and endurance. All you need to work muscles that are weak is ten minutes—that will make a big difference in your body alignment and form.

A muscle that carries out a specific movement is called the *prime mover*. The muscle that has the opposite action is the *antagonist*. Any other muscles that assist with the movement are called the *synergists*.

Try to maintain a good balance in the muscles by not overdeveloping the prime movers and neglecting the antagonists. For example, working the quadriceps (front of thighs) and not the hamstrings (back of thighs) creates an overdeveloped quadricep that could pave the way for a hamstring strain. Another example is working the pectorals (chest) and triceps (front of the upper arm), and not the trapezius or rhomboids (muscles in the back at the same level as the chest) or the triceps (back of the upper arm). This can keep you from enjoying good posture and may contribute to back pain.

While doing body-sculpting exercises, be sure you know which muscle you are working and what it is supposed to do. Knowing this will allow you to concentrate while you are strengthening and toning the muscle, providing better results and less chance of injury.

Injury can occur when you substitute other muscles for the one you are working, in order to compensate for fatigue or weakness in that muscle. If you can't maintain proper body alignment at all times, then you are working too hard and you need to do an easier version of the exercise.

Doing the movement slowly and with more control gives you time to examine your posture and form,

Snack Attack

When you're out and about and the urge hits, don't succumb to the junk-on-the-run syndrome. Do one of two things. Either take a healthy snack with you, or pick up something along the way.

Some examples of good portable snacks are bananas, apples, grapes, cherries, carrot slices, dried apricots, raisins, fruit juice, nuts, seeds, health bars, popcorn or whole-grain crackers or pretzels.

Or, if you pick up something healthy along the way—DO NOT pop into the quick-stop and head for the donuts. Instead go to a real grocery store and pick up any of the real food items listed above.

leading to a better workout. The first rule in avoiding poor form is to pull your abdominal muscles in tight through the entire exercise. This keeps the body stable, especially the spine and pelvis. Be sure not to hyper-extend the spine. It's better to do 10 moves correctly than 100 repetitions incorrectly. No matter what you're doing, you should never be in pain.

Abdominal strengthening

Probably the most important exercises you can do are those that help prevent back problems—abdominal strengthening exercises. *Abdominal curls* are best and almost everyone can do some form of them, no matter what their level of fitness.

For abdominal curls, lie on your back with knees up and feet flat on the floor. Lie down while doing exercises for the abdominals to lower your chance of injury to the lower back. Press the lower back to the floor by trying to touch your belly button to your spine. Bring your hands up to touch the knees as you lift your shoulders off the floor. Hold for one second and release. Do this slowly and with great control as many times as you can. If this position is easy for you, try the next level of difficulty—cross your arms over your chest as you lift your shoulders off the floor. If that is still easy for you, the *most* difficult is to put your hands behind your head as you lift your shoulders off the floor.

Be careful never to use your neck to do abdominal work. The abdominal muscles are the only ones that should be working. In fact, if you raise up more than about a 30 degree angle, you will be using the hip flexor muscles instead of the abdominals. The head doesn't bob up and down, but is in a straight line with the shoulders and the two move as a unit. Don't rely on momentum either, which puts strain on the neck. If you repeatedly do this exercise slowly and controlled, without letting the shoulders rest on the floor between contractions, you will firm your abdomen. This exercise won't cause you to lose fat—that can only be done by aerobics. It *will* firm the abdominal muscles, though, while fat is being lost.

Also important is strengthening the *oblique* muscles, those on either side of the abdominals, because they help keep the back stable, the abdomen pulled in and the waist defined. Toning them will help keep the waist small. To exercise the *obliques*, add a rotation to the abdominal curls described above. For example, as you raise your shoulders off the floor, rotate the upper body slightly to the left. Direct the right arm toward the opposite knee. Do this as many times as you can on one side and then repeat on the opposite side.

Buttocks, thighs and quadriceps

Pelvic tilts firm buttock muscles and can be done in the same position as the abdominal curls—lie on your back, knees bent, feet flat on floor, and press your belly button to your spine. Instead of lifting the upper torso, leave it flat on the floor and contract the buttock muscles as you tilt the pelvis toward you and lift it up no more than an inch or two off the floor. Hold for a second without arching the back, and slowly lower back down. Like the abdominal curls, this movement is small and controlled. Do as many as you can do correctly.

Another exercise to firm the buttock muscles is to get on your hands and knees with your back straight, not arched, and your abdomen pulled in tight. Your head should be in a straight line with your spine, not dropped down or arched back. Without leaning to one side or the other but staying balanced over both arms and legs, point your right leg straight out in back with your toe touching the floor. Lift the leg up to hip level and back down slowly. Be careful not to move anything but the leg and don't lift the leg higher than the hip because it compresses the vertical discs of the lower back. Repeat 10 to 30 repetitions on each leg.

For a *hamstring exercise*, a variation of the exercise described above, lift the leg to hip level, bend the knee and point the toe to the ceiling. In that position, lift up and down with little lifts of no more than two inches. Repeat on the opposite side.

For *side-lying leg lifts*, lie on your left side, keeping your body in a straight line with the hips not leaning to the front or back. Flex the right foot by bringing the toes toward the knees and lift your leg slowly up and down no more than six inches. If it's more comfortable for you, bend either or both legs. Repeat on the opposite side. Again, don't use momentum to throw the leg up and down, but do slow and controlled movements.

For *inner-thigh exercise*, stay in this same position on your left side. Bring your right leg over the left leg at a 45-degree angle to your body

Controlling Your Appetite with Exercise

Exercise helps curb your appetite, because the part of your brain that regulates body temperature is related to the area that affects appetite. When you raise your body temperature through exercise, your appetite decreases. That's why exercising during those hungry snack-attack hours in the mid-morning or late afternoon can be the key to controlling overall food consumption.

and rest it on the floor. Flex the left foot and lift and lower the left leg in a slow, controlled movement. Repeat on the opposite side. Remember to do the same number of repetitions on both sides.

Since hamstrings usually get a workout in the aerobic section, it's important to exercise opposing muscles—the *quadriceps*—equally. Lie on your back, prop up your upper torso on your elbows, pull your abdominals in tight, knees up, feet flat on the floor. Keeping the knees together, raise the right foot slowly until the leg is straight. Slowly lower until foot is on the floor. Repeat as many times as you are able, then do the same repetitions on the opposite leg. This exercise will strengthen muscles around the knee as well.

The Final Cool-down Stretch

There is a difference between the aerobic cool-down and the final cool-down stretch. The aerobic cool-down, which happens immediately after the aerobics exercise, gradually lowers your heart rate. By contrast, the cool-down stretch, at the end of the workout, emphasizes flexibility and relaxation. Since staying flexible becomes more important as we get older, these last few minutes in your exercise routine are a wise investment in your future.

During the final cool-down stretch, your body is thoroughly warmed up and ready to do the deep relaxing static stretching. You don't have to do difficult balancing, painful contractions, impressive double-jointed positions or even be particularly flexible to do static stretches. All you have to do is isolate the muscle and stretch it gently and slowly without requiring your body to be flexible at the joints as well. In fact, the fewer muscle groups you employ at one time, the less risk you have of injury. Remember to include all muscles you have worked, and try to hold your stretches for 10 to 30 seconds.

If you wish, you can take your heart-rate one final time after the stretching to see if you are below 60 percent of your maximum heart rate (the lowest number in your target heart rate zone). If you are not below this number, you have been working too hard and haven't spent enough time cooling down.

One last reminder: avoid hot showers or saunas immediately after you exercise. Because heat causes the blood to be drawn away from your heart and brain, *you must be completely cooled down first.*

Working Out With Weights

I once thought that working out with weights indicated an obsessive focus on body shape, as opposed to a healthy concern with health and fitness. I was wrong. The older I get, the more I see how essential working out with light weights is to total health. Most of us use only the front part of our arms and shoulders and neglect the muscles in the back of the arms and the upper back. Slumping at sedentary jobs eventually leads to rounded shoulders, which add years to our appearance— not to mention back stress. Strengthening muscles in the chest, shoulders, arms and upper back is crucial to good posture. I'm not talking about lifting 100-pound barbells, but rather, simple muscle strengthening with one to eight pound hand-held weights.

Since I started working out with five pound hand-held weights, three times a week for 10 to 20 minutes, I've noticed a remarkable difference in my strength. I can lift things I couldn't lift before without injury, and my posture has improved dramatically. I once thought the only way to have good posture was to force myself to stand up straight.

51

Unfortunately, when I wasn't thinking about it, I wasn't doing it. I've found, however, that when I do weight training and work the muscles in my upper back and arms, I *automatically* stand up straight, because my stronger muscles hold my torso erect. I don't even have to think about it.

Weight training also builds bones and strengthens joints. This is especially crucial for women as we get older because of the risk of osteoporosis after menopause and our increased fragility as we age. Experts recommend we start weight-bearing exercises in our 30s.

You could take 10 to 20 minutes at the end of your aerobic workout, after you've done the aerobic cool-down, to work with weights. Or you could do so after the final cool-down stretch. If you decide to work with weights on days when you are not doing aerobics, be sure to do at least a five-to-10-minute warm-up first, so muscles and joints are prepared and less susceptible to injury. I've found the best time for me to do weight work is immediately after the aerobic workout.

It's best to do weight training exercises on alternate days, but if you must do them every day, vary them so that you are not working the same muscles two days in a row. Why? Because muscles must have time to recover after each workout if they are going to build and strengthen. That rest in between is part of the strengthening process. This also helps avoid overtraining, which leads to weakness and injury.

Buy yourself two hand-held weights about two to eight pounds each. They should be light enough for you to easily do at least four repetitions of any exercise. They are too heavy if you can't do more than three repetitions. If you feel you can go on forever, you need to use heavier weights to increase the resistance. Work up to three sets of ten repetitions for each muscle you are working. Do it three times a week and within a month, you will see your muscles strengthen and take shape. When that becomes easy for you, increase the weight by one pound. If you stop for more than a week, decrease the weight or repetitions when you start again.

Muscular strength is best improved by doing *fewer* repetitions at a *higher* resistance. For example, when two-pound and three-pound weights became easy for me and I could do three sets of ten repetitions each with no problem, I changed to five-pound weights and back to five repetitions. If I had kept the same weights and only increased the repetitions, I would have increased my endurance, but not my muscle strength.

It's better to use free weights rather than ankle and wrist weights, because you can get a good grip on them and therefore have more control. Ankle and wrist weights are strapped on and used more for endurance training or to burn calories. They don't do much to increase strength or muscle mass. They help to increase muscle tone, but not muscle strength. Be careful with ankle and wrist weights, though, because carrying too much weight while you're doing other exercises puts a strain on the ankles, knees, hips and lower back.

The good news is that working out with weights increases lean body mass and decreases body fat. *Remember that lean body mass burns calories even when you are resting. So building muscle will at the same time help to decrease body fat.* This is important to keep in mind if you're trying to lose weight. If you have no muscle mass, you will miss out on that added means of burning calories.

Effective strength training depends on the *frequency* (how often), *duration* (how long), *intensity* (how hard) and degree of *resistance* (how much weight). It is best to know which muscle you are working and work it specifically in order to strengthen it. Working specific muscles (biceps, triceps, deltoids, pectorals, rhomboids, latissimus dorsi and trapezius) has made a remarkable difference in my upper-body strength and muscle definition. Previously a weak area for me, my wrists, arms, shoulders and back are more reliable and I am able to accomplish more without injury. I can now unscrew the tops of large glass jars, and I've come closer than ever to beating my 11-year-old at arm wrestling. (The advantages are endless!)

Best of all, strength training will strengthen your bones and help you avoid injury.

When you put together an exercise workout—whether with the help of a doctor, professional instructor, trainer or on your own—do it the right way. Avoid the pitfalls that can lead to injury and discouragement.

You're in this for *life*. Let's keep you happy and healthy on the way to a better body!

Chapter 4

Exercise Complications and Their Prevention

You exercise consistently for a week or so, and you feel your blood pulsing health and vitality to every cell. You sleep better, feel less daytime fatigue, and then, in the middle of a fun routine, *bang*, you experience injury. Sound familiar?

Injuries, stiffness and pain are major reasons people fail to turn good intentions to exercise into effective habits.

Can you avoid or minimize injury while exercising? *Yes.*

Problems that arise during exercise usually are caused by one of the following:

- not doing a thorough warm-up
- failure to increase intensity gradually
- working too hard, too long or too frequently(overuse)
- not paying attention to correct body form
- using improper body mechanics or exercise techniques
- neglecting a thorough cool-down
- wearing shoes that are ill-fitting and inappropriate for the activity
- working with faulty equipment

By far the most common exercise injury is *overuse,* or repeated stress to a part of the body over a period of time. Overuse most commonly occurs in the knees, legs, ankles, feet and lower back. Injury or stress frequently happens when beginning a new exercise program. Starting with high hopes of good results, we ignore the *less-is-more* warnings, and go full-speed ahead into exercising. When we end up with an injury, we get discouraged, turn in our aerobic shoes and go eat a bag of cookies. I hope to spare you from that.

No matter what shape you're in, you can overdo physical exercise. Don't exercise more than four days a week, unless you are working with professional trainers or know about cross-training and varying your workout. If you're a beginner, are out of shape or are starting to exercise after an illness or surgery, or if you've gone more than three weeks without exercising, don't do more than 20 minutes of low-intensity exercise every other day. *After two or more weeks,* increase intensity, duration or frequency gradually in order to prevent overuse injury.

There are two categories of exercise injuries—acute and chronic. An *acute injury* has a sudden onset. A *chronic injury* happens gradually, with no specific incident of injury, and can last weeks or months without getting better. Overuse is a chronic injury. If a chronic injury continues to be irritated and weakened, it can turn into an acute injury.

Symptoms of Overuse

Some signs of overuse or overtraining are pain, discomfort, weakness, burning, numbness, tingling or swelling any place in your body, but especially in the muscles, tendons and joints. If you feel exhausted or fatigued during or after exercise, if you have a marked increase in colds, flu or other illnesses, or if you have difficulty sleeping on the days when you exercise, reduce your exercise intensity, get plenty of rest and perhaps vary your physical activities.

Never ignore pain, whether it's specific pain, a dull general pain or a radiating pain. Whenever pain moves, comes and goes, or is accompanied by a tingling sensation, a nerve may be involved. Don't ignore muscle weakness, dizziness, nausea or blurred vision. Likewise, swelling always indicates too much stress on that body part. Black and blue discoloration means there is capillary damage and bleeding in the tissue.

Overuse injury occurs not only as a result of too much exercise, but also when the body doesn't have time to recover from the stress of the last exercise session. That's why it's best to work out every other day.

Another source of injury is overstretching a muscle without a proper warm-up, or warming up with ballistic stretches instead of static stretches. After a time off from exercise, I've occasionally pulled a muscle in my eagerness to get back to my regular routine.

An overuse injury also can happen if you use poor equipment. It's important that any equipment you use be in top condition. This includes shoes that are comfortable and that do not induce pain, discomfort, friction or pressure. They should absorb shock and impact, plus provide stability and support for the arches of your feet.

Feet, Knee, Leg and Back Injuries

Overuse injuries frequently occur in the legs and feet. Exercising for more than one hour, three to four times a week, increases your chance of injury. If within three days your pain and discomfort do not respond to ice packs, aspirin and rest, *see a doctor*. When you start to exercise again, allow yourself two weeks to get back in shape for every week lost due to injury. I've found it helpful when coming back from an injury to do rehabilitative exercises for the specific body parts that were weakened. I will briefly describe some common exercise injuries, so you can spot the symptoms in advance and take steps to prevent serious injury. Rather than providing reasons to avoid exercise, this discussion will encourage you to do it right.

Metatarsalgia

Metatarsalgia is an overuse injury caused by excessive weight-bearing or impact on the foot, in addition to failing to wear shoes that encourage proper foot alignment and arch support. The *metatarsal* bones in the foot bear all of our weight. A combination of too much impact on those bones and a high arch causes this area to break down.

57

Plan How You Will Quell "The Nibbles"

Keep healthy, easily accessible snacks in your refrigerator at all times for when you need a bite or two to quell a sudden onset of "the nibbles."

Place healthful snacks up-front, at eye level, in your refrigerator. Make it convenient to grab something good to satisfy that hunger pang.

Here's a tasty list (add your own favorites, too):
- *a bowl of grapes*
- *a bowl of cherries*
- *big, bright apples*
- *a heap of oranges*
- *sliced carrots or celery sticks*

This injury occurs gradually on repeated impact, usually from running or jumping, and can even result in a stress fracture.

When I was pregnant, carrying forty pounds of extra weight and exercising in shoes that gave inadequate support, I found myself with metatarsalgia. That was 17 years ago, before I learned the cause. A minor ache in the ball of my foot got worse until I could hardly walk. If I'd known as much as you will know when you finish reading this book, I wouldn't have ignored the pain so long before I sought help from a podiatrist. It took me nearly a year to recover, and even now I have to be careful of any high-impact movement.

Metatarsalgiac pain occurs in the ball of the foot and usually subsides when you stop exercising. If you experience this pain, stop your activity and apply ice to the affected area for 20 minutes several times a day. *When applying ice to an injured area, follow the instructions in the section called "Proper Icing" later in this chapter (page 62).* If pain persists after one to three days of self-treatment, see a podiatrist. With medical guidance, you can avoid an injury that can plague you for years to come.

Neuroma

Another problem caused by too much impact on the ball of the foot, plus wearing shoes that are too narrow and don't support the metatarsal area is neuroma. Unlike metatarsalgia, neuroma is characterized by sharp pain, caused by pressure on the interdigital nerves between the third and fourth toes. To prevent this type of injury, never do exercises on the ball of your foot or wear shoes that are too narrow.

See a doctor if pain persists beyond one to three days.

Plantar fasciitis

This injury is an inflammation of the connective tissue on the bottom of the foot. It is caused by overstretching the tissue where it attaches to the heel, and this is where the pain is felt. It can happen by pushing your weight onto the ball of the foot, the way a runner does, without proper warm-up. Arch supports, rest and icing the foot after any activity will help. As with most injuries, if pain persists beyond one to three days, see a doctor.

Stress fractures

Too much impact on a bone, occurring repeatedly, causes it to break down, leading to a stress fracture. Stress fractures can appear in any bone, but are most common in the metatarsal areas and in the *tibia*, or the bone of the lower leg.

In the beginning, the pain is gradual and goes away when you stop putting stress on the area. If you continue to exercise, the pain becomes sharp and constant, the area may swell and a fracture eventually occurs. Stress fractures happen gradually and don't always show up right away in an x-ray. If you have a stress fracture, you will notice a specific area that is painful and tender to touch.

To avoid stress fractures, do not do high-impact workouts on hard surfaces. Always increase exercise intensity gradually over a number of weeks, and wear supportive shoes with a shock-absorbing insole or orthotic. Whenever you feel pain, stop immediately and determine the cause. Substitute activities that are not weight bearing, such as swimming, bicycling or using a stationary bike, until you can resume your regular activities.

Tendinitis

Tendinitis, in the legs, results from repeated stretching or tearing of the achilles tendon, located in the back of the calf and attached to the heel. Most susceptible are people with poor muscle tone, or who have a lack of flexibility in that area, or who use improper foot form. Tendinitis usually comes on gradually, and in the beginning the pain is only felt *after* the activity. Later, the pain is chronic.

Avoid tendinitis with a proper warm-up, and with gentle stretching before and after any activity. Wearing high-heeled shoes all day and then putting on flat athletic shoes and exercising at full speed without stretching and warming up the muscles of your feet sets you up for injury. Again, good supportive shoes are important. Don't ever substitute *cheap* exercise shoes for *quality* ones. The moment you detect pain in the achilles area, rest from activity and apply ice.

Tendinitis is usually improved by rest—but don't let that make you inactive. If possible, see a doctor who specializes in sports medicine to help restore full use of your foot. The doctor can suggest stretching and strengthening exercises to prevent a recurrence, as well as prescribe an orthotic device if appropriate. This is one problem you do not have to live with. Don't let it limit you and cause you to neglect the exercise your body so badly needs.

Shin splints

Pain on the front or side of the lower legs, during and after exercise, usually indicates shin splints. There may or may not be a specific point of tenderness or swelling. The pain is caused by tight calf muscles, poor-supporting shoes, fallen arches, exercising on hard or unyielding surfaces, running incorrectly, poor foot form, not warming up sufficiently, overuse or progressing too quickly and intensely when working out. If you keep exercising with shin splints, they will turn into a stress fracture.

Prevent shin splints by wearing supportive shoes, avoiding high-impact or repeated moves on hard surfaces, properly warming up, increasing your exercise gradually, and strengthening the front shin muscles and stretching the calf muscles before you exercise.

Treatment for shin splints includes rest and applying ice several times a day.

Ankle sprains

Ligaments connect bone to bone. Ankle sprains result from stretching or tearing one or more ligaments at the ankle. A sprain can be as simple as a dull ache, or it can be severely painful, with swelling and black-and-blue discoloration.

I learned about sprains when I tore ligaments on both sides of my ankle. I didn't do it while exercising, skiing or skydiving, but when I slipped on a tile floor as I sought shelter from a rain storm.

There are three levels of sprains. A *first-degree* sprain means the ligament is stretched. *Second degree* indicates ligament fibers are torn. *Third degree* describes a ligament that is torn completely, in two or more places. My encounter with the slippery floor gave me a third-degree sprain, plus two fractures. I was in a cast and a brace for eight weeks, and I had to follow this with physical therapy for months.

Avoid exercise sprain by always wearing supportive shoes. The recommended treatment for an ankle sprain is "R.I.C.E." This stands for *rest, ice, compression* and *elevation*. In other words, get off your feet, put ice on the injured area for twenty minutes at a time (three to four times a day for 48–72 hours), wrap it snugly with an elastic wrap and raise it up above your heart so that fluid will drain from the injured area.

If you don't see improvement in one to three days, have the injury x-rayed to be certain there is no fracture. Wear a non-elastic ankle brace or tape the ankle for about six weeks following an injury.

Knee pain

Knee pain should never be ignored. Any knee injury—whether the result of a sudden twist, unstable foot form, hyperextension of the knees (pushed back), a sudden forced squat, or impact on the knee joint from any angle—can quickly become acute.

Prevent knee injury by conditioning and strengthening the hamstring muscles (back of leg) and quadricep muscles (front of leg) so they can better support the knee.

Pain can also result from chronic or gradual degeneration of the knee. An example is *chondromalacia*, where the cartilage in back of the kneecap becomes soft and rough, possibly due to poor lower body mechanics or running and jumping on hard surfaces.

Always see a doctor if knee problems last more than one to three days.

Back pain

Although back pain has many different causes, most frequently it is due to poor posture, weak abdominal muscles, tight hamstring muscles, poor body mechanics, congenital abnormalities, lack of flexibility, standing with knees hyperextended, excessively arching the back, lifting weights incorrectly or having a back injury. If you have any problems with your back, have a doctor advise you as to what exercises you can do.

Avoid back problems by keeping all your muscles strong—especially the muscles surrounding and supporting the back, such as the abdominals. Keep the hamstrings and the trunk flexible to help prevent stress in that area. Dislocation of our strongest joints—elbows, hips and ankles—is rare. Weaker joints—shoulders, intervertebral joints and knees—are more susceptible, so rely on strong ligaments and muscles to protect them. That's why it is important to strengthen the muscles surrounding the shoulders, the vertebra and the knees by doing exercises specifically for those purposes.

Proper icing

After I injured my ankle, I found it necessary to see a doctor who specializes in sports medicine. He taught me a lot about proper icing of an injury. Often, injured people apply ice incorrectly, and don't get the results they need—or worse, inflict further injury upon themselves. Here's how to apply ice properly:

First, *put ice on the injury as soon as possible.* Applying ice within minutes of the injury will keep swelling down, and help the injury heal more quickly. When an injury occurs, your body creates a protective splint—through swelling—around the damaged area to protect it from further injury. That swelling must go down before healing can happen.

Second, *do not put ice on the injured area for more than 10 to 20 minutes at a time.* This is enough time for blood vessels to constrict and decrease the blood flow, which decreases the swelling and pain. More time than that can freeze the tissue and cause serious, permanent damage.

Applying ice directly to the injured area (this method is referred to as "wet ice") works more effectively than placing a pack or bag of ice on the skin. *Don't submerge an injured body part in ice unless you are directed to do so by a doctor!*

Have wet ice on hand when you need it by filling small paper cups (about the size of a coffee cup) with water and then freezing them. Whenever you need it, take a cup out of the freezer, peel back the paper a little at a time and rub the ice over the injured area. Keep the ice moving. This method allows you to apply ice directly to the skin without freezing your fingers. And there is less danger of over-icing or frostbite because the ice melts in about 15 to 20 minutes. This method soothes the injured area—but keep the ice moving every second or two to prevent frostbite.

If you need to apply ice and don't have an ice-filled paper cup or any kind of ice pack on hand, try this. Put a small plastic bag inside another, fill it with ice (crushed ice is best), add a cup or two of water and tie the bag tightly shut.

Climate and Altitude Changes

It's also important to consider a few facts about exercising in different climates and altitudes. It can make a big difference to you or someone you know.

A tragic incident happened in the area where we live during a September heat wave. While training for high-school football, a teenager collapsed from heat-stroke and died. It sent shock waves through the community, especially

Avoid back problems by keeping all your muscles strong— especially the muscles surrounding and supporting the back, such as the abdominals.

affecting those of us who had sons on football teams.

The painful memory of that tragedy compels me to warn others of the potential dangers when exercising in hot weather.

Heat injury

Extreme heat most often affects the very young, the elderly, the overweight, the chronically ill and athletes. But heat injury can happen to anyone.

Exercise generates heat, drawing blood to the surface, where sweat forms on the skin and evaporates to cool the body. In hot weather, the body attempts to cool itself by sending excess blood to the surface of the skin, which reduces the amount of blood returning to the heart. Profuse sweating follows and a lot of body water is lost. If the water is not replaced, dehydration occurs, decreasing the amount of blood the heart pumps with each beat or stroke. As a result, the heart rate rises, leading to heat cramps, heat exhaustion or heatstroke.

Heat cramps, caused by excessive perspiration, most frequently occur in the calf, hamstring, quadricep and abdominal muscles. This fluid loss leads to dehydration, overheating and muscle fatigue. Prevent heat cramps by taking it easy when exercising until you have become acclimated to the warm weather. Drink plenty of water before, during and after exercise. Should heat cramps occur, stop exercising, stretch out the part of the body that is cramping, apply cold moist towels to the area and drink cool water.

Heat exhaustion, the next level of injury from overworking in the heat, also is marked by excessive sweating, leading to water and salt depletion and a decrease in blood volume. When the weather is hot, blood flow to the skin increases to help dissipate heat through sweating. Exercising requires more blood to bring oxygen to the working muscles. Since the brain and the heart still need as much blood as usual, heat exhaustion occurs if the cardiovascular system can't meet this extra demand for blood.

Symptoms of heat exhaustion are weakness, dizziness, fainting, headaches, nausea and vomiting, pale skin, profuse sweating and a weak but rapid pulse. Treatment must be immediate. Stop exercising, drink plenty of cool water, put a cool, damp cloth on your head, face and neck—*and get to a doctor immediately.* You may require an intravenous solution to replace fluid loss.

Heatstroke is by far the most serious heat injury. Because there is a high mortality rate associated with heat stroke, it should be treated as a medical emergency. Heatstroke indicates that the body's cooling system has failed. Body temperature rises to a level that damages the brain and spinal cord, and can quickly lead to death. Heatstroke can occur suddenly, or it can progress as the next stage after heat exhaustion.

Due to the central nervous system's inability to function in heatstroke, symptoms include seizures, coma, confusion, odd behavior and a glassy stare. The skin becomes red, hot and dry, because sweating has shut down to prevent further dehydration. The pulse becomes fast and strong, and the pupils of the eyes are small.

Recovery from heatstroke depends on how quickly body temperature can be brought down to normal. Call immediately for Emergency Medical Services, or if it is quicker, take the victim to an emergency hospital. At the same time, remove the victim's clothing so the skin is exposed. Immerse

Digestive Enzymes

Without an adequate supply of digestive enzymes in your body, you can eat the purest and best food available and still not retain enough nutrients to benefit you. Digestive enzymes help break down food so it is fully absorbed into the system. Whenever we are under stress, taking certain medications or experiencing chemical imbalances in our bodies, our supply of enzymes are drastically affected. The supply also diminishes as we age.

An ineffective amount of digestive enzymes could be keeping your body feeling starved, exhausted and sickly day after day. There are natural aids to digestion, like fresh papaya, fresh pineapple and honey, which pass into your bloodstream rapidly. But sometimes even those foods are not enough, and we need to take digestive enzyme supplements. This is especially true for people who are highly stressed or over age 50. If you feel this might benefit you, check with a doctor, nutritionist or expert who can recommend a good natural enzyme supplement.

them in cool water, or put cool, damp towels or cloths on their skin.

Always act immediately if you suspect heatstroke. Every minute counts.

Heat and humidity

A combination of heat and humidity can be dangerous, because sweat will not evaporate easily and the body doesn't cool. If you must do any kind of physical activity in hot, humid weather, greatly reduce the intensity of exercise until you have become acclimated. In fact, when doing *any* kind of physical work in high temperature and humidity, give your body time to adjust. It takes five to ten days to acclimatize yourself to those conditions. When you begin physical work in high heat and humidity, do only half as much work as you normally would do. Increase your work time gradually.

When exercising in heat or humidity, wear lightweight clothes with good ventilation, exercise slowly to allow your body to acclimate and continually replace lost fluids. Prevent dehydration by drinking eight to 10 ounces of water, about 10 to 20 minutes before working out. If exercising in extreme heat or for a prolonged period of time, take breaks every 15 minutes to drink more water. Spray your skin with water to help cool it, and avoid saunas, hot tubs or hot showers after exercise.

I made the young football player in my family read this section on heat injury. Please do the same with anyone you know who could be at risk. By following these guidelines, a disaster can be prevented.

Exercising in cold weather

The greatest dangers of exercising in cold weather are chilling and dehydration. Allow for adequate ventilation of sweat by wearing layers of clothing and a hat. Wear clothes made of fabrics that allow heat to be released during exercise and retained heat when resting. You can easily become chilled after exercising, so put on warm clothing immediately. Even though the weather is chilly, and it doesn't seem as if you are sweating much, you can still become dehydrated. Be sure to replace body fluids that have been lost by drinking plenty of water.

Exercising in high altitudes

High altitudes reduce the oxygen-carrying capacity of the blood, so you can't get as much oxygen to the muscles. As a result, you must reduce your exercise intensity or duration. Be sure to do an extended gradual warm-up and cool-down. In high altitudes, you may develop headaches and it may take several months to acclimate yourself, so go slowly and *don't push it.*

Listen To Your Heart

If you smoke, have high cholesterol, high blood pressure or a family history of heart disease, you must have a medical checkup and release from your doctor before exercising. Call a doctor immediately if you experience any of these symptoms: chest pain, dull ache or pressure in the chest, irregular heartbeat, palpitations or sudden breathlessness. To avoid problems, pay special attention to warm-ups and cool-downs.

Myocardial infarction

Also known as heart attack, myocardial infarction is life-threatening. Symptoms include sudden weakness, sweating, nausea, abnormal heartbeat and faintness. There can also be a crushing pain in the chest, between the shoulder blades, radiating to the jaw, down the left arm or both arms, that can last over 30 minutes. If these symptoms are evident, stop physical activity and call immediately for emergency medical help.

Angina pectoris

This condition, usually brought on by emotional stress or physical exercise, indicates an insufficient supply of blood and oxygen to the heart. The pain in the chest feels like a heart attack, but is relieved when enough oxygen reaches the heart. This is usually accomplished by resting or taking *nitroglycerin.* The pain lasts anywhere from seconds to a few minutes, but because the heart muscle is not destroyed, death does not follow. Because the chest pain is similar to a heart attack, don't diagnose yourself or anyone else. Call immediately for emergency medical help at the first sign of chest pain.

I've issued a lot of warnings here, but you need not let any of these exercise complications keep you from a healthy workout. Instead, let them be a motivation to exercise *properly*.

Our bodies must have exercise. Just make sure you are doing what's right for *you*.

Chapter 5

Food Is Not Our Enemy

What gives you the most problems when working on better body management? For most of us, it is what we eat. But food never was intended to be our enemy, and we were not meant to struggle with it as we do. Before there were processed convenience foods, we had vegetable gardens, fruit orchards and whole grains. We ate fresh meat, chicken, fish, turkey and lamb. And there were few problems with obesity. Today we can eat whatever we want, any time we want it—and that's what we do. Then, after we watch the scale go up, we get panicked or disgusted with ourselves and try anything to get rid of the weight—even unhealthy gimmicks, fads and diets.

We were created to eat a variety of fresh, natural foods, but that can be difficult for most of us. We tend to fixate on a few foods and crave them above all others. The good news is our taste buds *can* be re-trained once we see the benefits of better eating for a better body.

Food serves three purposes for us: 1) it provides adequate fuel so our bodies will have ample energy, 2) its nutrients repair damaged tissue and facilitate the growth of new tissue,

Next to oxygen, the most important element for sustaining life is water.

and 3) it stimulates metabolic functions that help our bodies operate efficiently and effectively.

Beyond that, food is what we make it to be. Sure, food is enjoyable and a means of celebration, but there are more important purposes for food than titillating our taste buds and providing emotional comfort. We can learn to eat healthfully, allowing food to accomplish its three purposes in us. Learning to eat for *health* rather than for consolation and entertainment will give us the results we desire.

What Are the Basic Nutrients?

The basic nutrients we need are water, protein, fats, carbohydrates, vitamins and minerals. Our responsibility is to take in the right amount of each nutrient. When you have an adequate supply of each in proper balance, you set the stage for health and good body composition. But good health and proper body weight cannot come from diet or exercise alone. You must have both, in proper balance; energy output must be balanced by fuel intake, and fuel intake must include a balance of basic nutrients.

Adequate Hydration

Of all the nutrients your body needs, water most constantly needs replenishing. Next to oxygen, it is the most important element for sustaining life. Every cell in your body needs water to function. Water contributes to body form, regulates body temperature and aids in elimination of waste products.

Thirst is not an adequate indicator of the body's need for water. Instead, consider how much water you are taking in, and how much you are expending. When exercising and sweating profusely, we can lose a lot of water and yet not feel thirsty. So it's good to have a system or schedule for drinking water. Because we need a whopping 64 ounces of water daily, try breaking it into four segments:

• Drink 16 ounces at least one hour before breakfast.
• Drink 16 ounces at least one hour before lunch.
• Drink 16 ounces at least one hour before dinner.
• Drink 16 ounces at least one hour before bedtime.

Adhering to this schedule sustains normal bodily functions. If you experience water loss due to strenuous physical activity, you need even more water.

When we exercise, we eliminate body heat through perspiration. The body can perspire about a half a quart per hour without a problem. But when we exceed that amount without replacing it, the blood cannot circulate as well and body temperature regulation suffers. Becoming even slightly dehydrated stresses the cardiovascular system, increases the heart rate and elevates body temperature. If you become overheated, it could make exercising so difficult that you forgo it altogether. (Here's one frustration and discouragement that has a simple answer.) Dehydration is serious and must never be taken lightly. First, follow the drinking schedule above. Then, make sure you drink a cup of water before exercising, every 15 minutes during strenuous exercise, and after exercising. Drinking adequate amounts of water will keep your core temperature down, maintain your blood volume and reduce the stress on your cardiovascular system.

Cold water quenches thirst best. It leaves the stomach more quickly than warm drinks do, and it cools the body more efficiently. Liquids with sugar in them prevent the water from being absorbed as quickly into the system. Usually, only five percent of a sugar drink is absorbed 15 minutes after drinking it; 70 percent of plain water is absorbed by that time. A drink containing sucrose, glucose and fructose is not going to do you much good when you are exercising.

Water always is the best choice.

Protein In Moderation

Protein is a major requirement for better bodies—we must have it to grow and repair cells. It is not generally a source of fuel for energy, except when our calorie intake is so low that it doesn't meet the body's fuel needs. There are twenty amino acids found in protein, and nine of them are considered essential to health. Meat, fish and poultry, dairy products and eggs contain all nine and are *complete proteins*. All others—grains, legumes, seeds and nuts—are *incomplete proteins*, though grains and legumes *together* make a complete protein.

Protein makes up about half of the dry weight of the body. It helps to form hormones and enzymes, and is vital to the brain and nervous system. It makes up blood proteins like albumin, fibrinogen, globulin, hemoglobin and gamma globulin.

Because protein is our primary building material, it pays to get it as purely and as unprocessed as possible. So stay away from processed meat, or meat with chemicals in it. Because poultry, fish and lamb are more easily digested than beef and pork, it's good to eat more of those protein sources.

In order to avoid a diet too high in protein, try not to eat meat more than once a day. Because meat takes 24 hours to move through the digestive system, wait two to three hours after you eat it before you exercise.

The American Council on Exercise recommends that only about 12 percent of our food intake be protein. (Carbohydrates should be about 58 percent, and fat should be about 30 percent.) Most people eat a lot more protein than that—and more fat, too. Too much protein produces excess nitrogen, and forces the kidneys and liver to work overtime to get rid of it. I'm not suggesting we all be vegetarians, but we do our bodies a big favor when we take in a moderate amount of protein. Any excess protein will be stored as *fat*.

Aside from meat, other sources of protein are eggs, lowfat milk and cheese. These three foods are the focus of periodic battles in the health industry. Some nutritionists would have us drink a gallon of milk and eat a pound of cheese a day, to meet our need for calcium. Others tell us not to eat dairy products, because they are hard to digest—and, besides, we're the only species that drinks milk after we're grown. Some experts say no eggs whatsoever because of the cholesterol; others say eggs are a whole food that contains lecithin, which balances the cholesterol in the body. I say, unless you are allergic to dairy products or eggs, *be balanced and wise.* I don't exclude any of these from my diet, nor do I tank-up on them either.

Seeds and nuts also are a great source of protein, but unless they are broken down into butters (such as peanut butter), we often don't chew them well enough to digest them easily. Get the best benefit from nuts and seeds by selecting pure, unprocessed and uncooked varieties and chewing them well.

You'll need more protein if you are healing from an illness or injury, if you are pregnant or nursing or if you are growing. If you aren't getting enough carbohydrates to fuel your workouts, protein provides extra energy.

How much protein do I need?

The average adult needs about *.36 grams* of protein per pound of body weight. Find out how much protein you need by multiplying your body weight by .36. For example:

	My Weight	YourWeight
Body Weight:	120 lbs.	____ lbs.
Multiplied by:	x .36	x .36
Total grams needed:	43.20	

I need: <u>43</u> grams   You need: __ grams

You don't have to get into weighing your food and counting your grams every meal, but I want you to be generally aware of your needs. Use the Protein Gram Chart (Chart A) to determine whether you are getting too much protein or too little. The chart lists the most common sources of protein with the highest gram content, to give you an idea how much protein you are eating.

Cutting Down On Fats

Yes, your body needs *some* fat. But as with protein, most of us eat more fat than we require.

We need fat as a source of energy, to carry fat-soluble vitamins to the cells, to contribute to the myelin sheath that covers our nerves and for our only source of linoleic acid, which promotes healthy skin. Fat also is necessary for hormone production, and to insulate and protect our organs from rapid heat loss. Fat, also called *lipids*, is insoluble in water and combines with other nutrients to form blood lipids, cell membranes, digestive bile and Vitamin D. Since fat can be metabolized as an energy source, it is of special interest to those of us who want to lose weight. I will go into greater detail about that in the next chapter, "Controlling Body Fat."

There is much talk today about different types of fat. If you're like me, you get confused when reading labels. There are two types of fat—*animal fat*, which is saturated fatty acids and cholesterol, and *plant fat*, which is unsaturated fatty acids. *Saturated fat* comes from animal sources, is solid at room temperature and *raises cholesterol* in your blood.

Unsaturated fat comes from plant sources, is liquid at room temperature and *lowers cholesterol*. Unsaturated fats from plant sources are either mono-unsaturated or polyunsaturated. *Polyunsaturated* indicates an oil whose molecules consist of carbon chains with *many* double bonds, unsaturated by hydrogen atoms. Don't you feel better knowing that? Actually, all you really need to know is this: unsaturated and polyunsaturated fats are the good guys; saturated fats are the bad guys that contribute to heart disease.

Try to keep your fat intake to no more than 30 percent of your total calories, and at least two-thirds of that should be unsaturated fat. Reduce fat in your diet by eating mostly chicken, turkey and fish. Keeping meat portions small, cutting off any fat and broiling or roasting rather than frying eliminates a lot of fat. Use polyunsaturated oils instead of saturated fat for cooking, avoid highly processed cheese and butter and eat low-fat or non-fat dairy products rather than whole milk or whole cheese. Fill up on fruits, vegetables, whole grains, berries, nuts and seeds.

Carbohydrates as Fuel

Power and energy for physical activity is most readily available from carbohydrates. Carbohydrates break down into a simple sugar called *glucose*, which is your body's primary immediately usable source of energy. Additionally, glucose helps the body burn fat more efficiently. While glucose is stored in the muscle tissue and liver, it is called *glycogen*. You can't maintain an adequate level of glycogen without carbohydrates.

There are two kinds of carbohydrates—simple and complex. *Simple carbohydrates* are refined and found in sugar and sweets. They provide a short-term energy source without any nutritional contribution. *Complex carbohydrates* are found in fruits, vegetables, whole grains and beans. They contain fiber, which aids in elimination. Nearly 60 percent of our food intake should come from complex carbohydrates. When you sit down to eat, is half the food on your plate fruits, vegetables, whole grains or beans?

Stop Being Hard On Yourself

Too often we beat ourselves up for the way we look, feel or behave, when actually the problem is a physiological imbalance. Although it may not be serious enough to show up in a medical exam, even a relatively minor chemical alteration can throw off sleep patterns, appetite, emotions or the way we digest, process and absorb food. This could leave us feeling dull, tired, depressed, unfocused, forgetful, anxious, even fearful and angry. Any number of physical changes could cause this. Instead of condemning yourself, assuming you're a hypochondriac or resorting to artificial substances to alleviate symptoms, check with an expert in the field of body care to see if you are vitamin or mineral deficient. It could be that your body is changing through the natural growth and aging process, and all you need to do is make a few habit adjustments.

Vitamins and Minerals

Our bodies cannot produce vitamins, but they are vital to growth, maintenance, tissue repair and reproduction. Vitamins are divided into two groups: *Water-soluble vitamins* C and B are not stored in the body, so they must be replaced regularly. *Fat-soluble vitamins* A, D, E and K are stored in body fat and in the liver. Because fat-soluble vitamins are potentially toxic, there is a danger of overdosing.

Vitamins are gaining favor these days, a far cry from the recent past when their value was questioned. Now the controversy is not over whether vitamins have value, but whether their sale should be regulated and restricted.

Store-bought vitamins have value for those who find it difficult to get the balanced diet they need. Nevertheless, vitamins are best absorbed when obtained through the food we eat, preferably raw or lightly cooked and unprocessed. Vitamin and mineral supplements should never be a substitute for a healthy diet. Get advice from an expert on the best way to take vitamins.

The Vitamin Chart (see Chart B) lists good food sources for each vitamin as well as how they affect the body. Rather than worrying about how many milligrams you are getting, eat a variety of the foods listed on that chart and you will do well.

Minerals are vitally important in conducting nerve impulses, and growing and maintaining healthy bones, teeth, hormones and hemoglobin. They also aid in blood clotting, controlling certain body reactions and production of energy. Minerals require no digestion as they are absorbed directly from the small intestine.

There are two types of minerals: *major minerals* and *trace minerals*. Major minerals are needed in large amounts; trace minerals are needed in smaller quantities. Major minerals include calcium, phosphorus, magnesium, potassium, sulfur, sodium and chloride. Some trace minerals are iron, copper, iodine, cobalt, zinc fluoride, manganese, selenium and chromium.

Don't drive yourself crazy trying to determine if you are getting enough of each mineral. It's better to look at the foods listed with each mineral on the Major Mineral Chart (see Chart C) and Trace Mineral Chart (Chart D) and rotate those foods into your diet every few weeks.

If you eat a variety of pure, fresh foods, you will get all the vitamins and minerals you need. If you must exclude certain foods from your diet (dairy products, meat, specific grains or certain vegetables and fruits), make sure you are getting the vitamins and minerals contained in that food from another food or a food supplement. No vitamin pill can substitute for food, but it *can* help supplement what is missing.

Calcium

One of the most important major minerals is calcium, because it is found in the greatest quantity in our bodies. A 150-pound person will have nearly three-and-a-half pounds of calcium in his or her body. Ninety-nine percent of the calcium in our bodies is in our bones and teeth, with a small amount in the bloodstream. Too little calcium causes weak bones and other maladies.

We need at least 800 milligrams of calcium a day, but it's best not to rely entirely on pasteurized milk as your source. An adult may find that drinking enough milk to supply that need is too much. Other good sources of calcium include broccoli, spinach, salmon and lentils. (See the Good Food Sources list under Calcium on the Major Minerals Chart.) It's good to have a wide variety of calcium-rich foods in your diet. Additionally, plenty of exercise in the fresh air and sunshine will keep you calcium-healthy.

Iron

One of the most important trace minerals is iron, because it is essential to life. We need iron to produce hemoglobin, which carries oxygen in the blood. With too little hemoglobin, our muscles don't get enough oxygen and we have little energy or endurance. In an extreme case, we could suffocate from a lack of oxygen in the blood and die. Without adequate amounts of iron, hemoglobin and oxygen, our body cannot rid itself of waste material and toxins. Circulation, digestion and elimination suffer as well. Without proper amounts of iron and oxygen, we can't maintain body heat and will feel cold all the time. Muscles generate heat when oxygen is circulating in them, so exercising regularly through the winter will help keep you warmer.

We can become iron deficient due to: blood loss through injury or heavy menstrual flow, overtraining, perspiring heavily without fluid replacement, and inadequate iron intake or absorption. You can increase your iron level by eating dark leafy green vegetables, prunes, raisins, dried apricots, strawberries, legumes or other foods listed on the Trace Mineral Chart. Cook in cast-iron pots and pans for extra iron, and because it aids iron absorption, take vitamin C or eat foods rich in vitamin C. Intense heat destroys iron, so cook food containing iron lightly.

Women need more iron than men, and pregnant and nursing women need even more. But don't self-prescribe iron. Check with a doctor to determine the amount you need.

The vitamin and mineral charts at the end of this chapter are meant to provide *guidelines*, not to overwhelm you with counting milligrams. Even if all you have time for is scanning the column called Good Food Sources to see if you are getting a good variety of all those foods on a regular basis, you still would benefit. And you need not rush to the grocery store and buy everything on the list—just make sure you are getting a good representation each week from each of the food sources.

The recommended daily requirement of each vitamin and mineral is not given, because I want to encourage you to get them from your food. The point is to know the type and quantity of foods to eat, and hopefully, you will be inspired to eat a wide variety. The benefits are worth the effort.

Say *No* To These Foods

Some foods not only harm our bodies, but also take up room in our digestive track that could be filled by foods that are good for us. To live healthfully, avoid these foods: refined foods, sugar, white flour, white rice, fat and caffeine.

Refined foods

Sometimes it's not the food that is to blame, but what has been *done* to it. In an effort to preserve food longer and make it more pleasing to the eye and appealing to the taste buds, we have bleached, dyed, stripped, flavored and chemicalized food to death—*literally*. We process out the vitamins, minerals and enzymes, and add harmful chemicals.

We buy and eat food without any life in it. Many illnesses are a result of eating dead foods. Before you put any food in your mouth, determine how pure it is, how fresh and how close it is to its original state. Processed food provides taste and calories—but few nutrients.

Sugar

The calories in white sugar convert directly to fat, and provide no nutrients. Perhaps even worse, the more sugar you eat, the less you desire good food. To help control your sugar craving, try substituting fruit or honey for sugar. These will satisfy a sweet tooth, but are digested quickly and contain nutrients. Avoid sugar—except for special occasions.

Sugar promotes tooth decay and takes calcium and vitamin B out of your system, leading to nerve and heart problems, constipation, low blood sugar, fatigue and headaches. Watch the artificial sweeteners too. They contribute no nutrients to the body, but what they do contribute is still highly suspect.

It is a myth that consuming sugar before exercising will give you energy. It may give you a quick rush due to the increase in blood sugar, but as that level falls, you will feel weak and tired and your performance actually will be impaired. You will be able to exercise for less time before becoming exhausted.

White flour and white rice

Refining wheat and rice has left these grains without any of their original nutrients. The refining process strips away the germ of the grain, leaving it bleached and devitalized. With the vitamins and minerals removed, you are left with food your body has to struggle to get rid of. But there is little energy to do that, because you haven't been strengthened with nutrients. Instead, eat whole-grain cereal, bread and brown rice, to provide your body vitamin- and mineral-rich carbohydrates.

Caffeine

Caffeine stimulates the central nervous system and the heart, and contributes to sleep problems, nervousness, high blood pressure, ulcers, muscular unsteadiness and an overly acidic system. Too much acid in the blood causes the body to retain water in an attempt to neutralize it. This adds weight. Although it is best to avoid caffeine altogether, avid coffee, tea, chocolate or cola consumers may not want to give it up completely. At least cut down on your caffeine intake—I guarantee you will benefit from it.

Fat

As we've seen, we do need *some* fat. But most of us are not suffering from a fat deficiency. Usually that occurs only in people who suffer from anorexia or are starving. Be sure that your intake of fat foods is *minimal*. More about that in the next chapter on controlling body fat.

What follows are guidelines that will help you design your own better body food plan.

(Don't skip over them!)

	Protein Source	Approximate Measurement	Protein Grams
	Cow's milk (whole)	1 quart	32
	Cow's milk (skim)	1 quart	36
	Yogurt (low fat)	1 cup	8
	Cottage cheese	1 cup	38
	Cheddar cheese	1/2 cup	14
	Swiss cheese	1 oz.	7
	Eggs	2	12
	Roast beef	3 oz.	16
	Lean ground beef	3 oz.	24
	Steak (sirloin)	3 oz.	20
	Chicken breast	3 oz.	25
	Lamb chop	4 oz.	24

Chart A

Protein

Grams

Source	Measurement	Grams
Pork chop	3 1/2 oz.	16
Turkey	3 1/2 oz.	27
Halibut	3 1/2 oz.	26
Salmon	3 oz.	17
Swordfish	1 steak	27
Tuna (canned)	3 oz.	25
Red kidney beans	1 cup	15
Brussels sprouts	1 cup	12
Lentils	1 cup	15
Split-pea soup	1 cup	6
Soybeans	1 cup	22
Whole-wheat bread	1 slice	2
Yellow corn meal	1 cup	9
Whole wheat flour	1 cup	13
Macaroni & cheese	1 cup	18
Oatmeal	1 cup	5
Buckwheat pancakes	4 small	7
Popcorn	2 cups	3
Rice (brown)	1 cup	15
Spaghetti/meat cauce	1 cup	13
Wheat germ	1 cup	17
Bean soup	1 cup	8
Almonds	1/2 cup	13
Brazil nuts	1/2 cup	10
Peanut butter	1/2 cup	13
Sesame seeds	1/2 cup	9
Sunflower seeds	1/2 cup	12
Walnuts	1/2 cup	7

Chart B

Vitamins

VITAMIN A
How It Affects The Body
- Is fat soluble.
- Makes tissues resistant to colds, fights infection, important to health of eyes, bones, skin and teeth.
- Is stored in the body so it can be overdosed.
- Is depleted under stress.
- Is destroyed by overcooking.

Good Food Sources
avocados, cabbage, cantaloupe, carrots, celery, cherries, dried apricots, egg yolks, endive, leaf lettuce, liver, melons, whole milk, papayas, peaches, prunes, spinach, sweet potatoes, tomatoes, yellow and green leafy vegetables, yellow squash

VITAMIN B
How It Affects The Body
- Is water soluble.
- Normalizes the brain and nervous system, increases metabolic processes.
- Promotes healthy skin, hair, eyes, mouth and liver.
- Helps absorption of food.
- A lack of Vitamin B causes nervous exhaustion, dull hair, skin and eyes, and fatigue.

Good Food Sources
almonds, avocados, beef, broccoli, dairy products, dates, eggs, fish, leafy green vegetables, legumes, liver, onions, peanuts, peas, peppers, pork, potatoes, poultry, prunes, spinach, walnuts, wheat germ, whole grain cereals and breads

VITAMIN C
How It Affects The Body
- Is water soluble.
- Strengthens blood vessels and helps strengthen and heal the body.
- A lack of Vitamin C causes tender gums, poor complexion, loss of energy, nosebleeds and slow healing.
- Not stored in the body so must be replaced every day.

Good Food Sources
  apples, berries, broccoli, cabbage, cauliflower, citrus fruits, cucumbers, endive, green peppers, melons, parsley, peas, spinach, strawberries, tomatoes, watercress

VITAMIN D
How It Affects The Body
- Is fat soluble.
- Helps to absorb calcium and phosphorus and build bones.
- Regulates mineral metabolism and stabilizes the nervous system.

Good Food Sources
  egg yolk, fish oil, fish, green leafy vegetables, milk (another good source is sunshine on the skin)

VITAMIN E
How It Affects The Body
- Is fat soluble.
- Necessary for reproduction, lactation and menstrual health.
- Protects red blood cells, prevents blood clots and helps to heal wounds.

Good Food Sources
  green leafy vegetables, milk, nuts, vegetables oils, wheat germ, whole grains, yellow corn

VITAMIN F

How It Affects The Body
- Is fat soluble.
- Aids in growth, healthy hair and nails, and good skin, and contributes to nerve health.

Good Food Sources
eggs, fruits, nuts, spinach, vegetables oils, whole grains

VITAMIN K

How It Affects The Body
- Is synthesized by plants and stored in the liver.
- Helps to clot the blood.

Good Food Sources
cabbage, cauliflower, leafy green vegetables, milk, tomatoes, wheat bran

Chart C

Major

Minerals

CALCIUM

How It Affects The Body
- Important to the formation of strong bones and teeth, the clotting of blood, and production of energy
- Also helps the nerves and muscles to function properly.

Good Food Sources
almonds, avocados, barley, blackstrap molasses, broccoli, brown rice, brussels sprouts, buckwheat, cabbage, carrots, cauliflower, cheese, coconut, cornmeal, egg yolk, figs, fish, gelatin, greens, kelp, lentils, milk, millet, oats, onions, prunes, rye, sesame seeds, soy milk, walnuts, watercress, whole wheat

CHLORIDE

How It Affects The Body
- Aids in the function of muscles and nerves.

Good Food Sources
most protein foods

MAGNESIUM

How It Affects The Body
- Calms the nerves and aids in nerve transmissions.
- Neutralizes and helps to eliminate poisons.
- Is important to proper heart function.

Good Food Sources
apples, apricots, avocados, bananas, beet tops,

brown rice, cabbage, coconuts, corn, cornmeal, dates, endive, figs, fish, gelatin, grapes, green pepper, goat milk, honey, lentils, mint, nuts, oats, parsley, peas, peaches, pears, prunes, rye, soybeans, spinach, sunflower seeds, tofu, watercress, whole wheat

PHOSPHORUS
How It Affects The Body
- Crucial to development of strong bones and teeth and nourishment for the brain and nerves.

Good Food Sources
almonds, barley, beans, bone broth, brown rice, cabbage, carrots, cashew nuts, corn, dairy products, egg yolk, fish, kelp, lentils, millet, oats, olives, pecans, pumpkin seeds, rye, sardines, sesame seeds

POTASSIUM
How It Affects The Body
- Aids in elimination, circulation, brain and nervous function.
- Is important for the production of energy.

Good Food Sources
almonds, apples, apple cider vinegar, apricots, bananas, beans, beets, black cherries, blueberries, broccoli, brussels sprouts, carrots, cashews, cucumbers, currants, dates, egg whites, figs, fish, goat milk, grapes, kale, leaf lettuce, lentils, lima beans, olives, parsley, pears, pecans, potato peeling, raisins, rice bran, sesame seeds, soybeans, spinach, sunflower seeds, swiss chard, tomatoes, turnips, walnuts, watercress, wheat bran, wheat germ

SODIUM

How It Affects The Body
- Good for muscles and nerves.
- Promotes pliable joints. Affects brain functions and metabolism.

Good Food Sources

apples, apricots, asparagus, barley, beets, cabbage, celery, cheeses, coconut, dairy products, dates, egg yolks, figs, fish, goat milk, greens, horseradish, kale, kelp, lentils, okra, parsley, peas, prunes, raisins, seafood, sesame seeds, spinach, strawberries, sunflower seeds, swiss chard, turnip

SULFUR

How It Affects The Body
- Feeds hair, skin and nails,and has an important influence on the liver.
- Regulates nerve impulses.
- Although the drug form of sulfur can cause adverse reactions, food with sulfur in it doesn't cause problems.

Good Food Sources

almonds, anise seeds, apples, apple cider vinegar, apricots, bananas, beans, beets, black cherries, blueberries, broccoli, brussels sprouts, carrots, cashews, cucumbers, currants, dates, egg whites, figs, fish, goat milk, grapes, kale, kelp, leaf lettuce, lentil, lima beans, olives, parsley, pears, pecans, potato peeling, raisins, rice bran, sesame seeds, soybeans, spinach, sunflower seeds, tomatoes, turnips, walnuts, watercress, wheat bran, wheat germ

Chart D

Trace

Minerals

CHROMIUM
How It Affects The Body
- Enhances the performance of insulin and contributes to the control of blood sugar.

Good Food Sources
yeast, liver, whole grains, meat, cheese, peas, corn oil, and cloves

COBALT
How It Affects The Body
- Important to the formation of red blood cells.

Good Food Sources
apricots, meat, oysters, clams, sea vegetation, goat milk

COPPER
How It Affects The Body
- Aids formation of red blood cells and bones.
- Increases iron assimilation.

Good Food Sources
liver, kidney, seafood, nuts, raisins, legumes, whole-grain cereals

IODINE
How It Affects The Body
- Important for normal growth and development, reproduction and lactation.

Good Food Sources

    artichokes, asparagus, beans, blueberries, brussels sprouts, carrots, chives, coconut, cucumber, egg
      plant, fish, garlic, goat milk, green peppers, leaf lettuce, oats, okra, onions, peanuts, potatoes, spinach, squash, strawberries, tofu, tomatoes, turnips, watercress, watermelon

IRON

How It Affects The Body

- Produces hemogloblin, carries oxygen in the blood and releases it to the tissues.
- Helps prevent anemia.

Good Food Sources

    almonds, apricots, bananas, blackberries, black cherries, blackstrap molasses, dates, dried fruits, egg yolk, green leafy vegetables, legumes, lentils, lima beans, liver, meat, millet, nuts, organ meat, parsley, peaches, peas, pinto beans, prunes, pumpkin seeds, raisins, red beans, rye, soybeans, spinach, sprouted seeds and beans, sunflower seeds, white beans (dried), whole-grain cereal and bread

MANGANESE

How It Affects The Body

- Contributes to bone growth, fat metabolism and reproduction.
- Feeds nerves and brain.

Good Food Sources

    almonds, apples, apricots, blackberries, blackeyed peas, blueberries, celery, chestnuts, green beans, leaf lettuce, mint, oats, parsley, pineapple, walnuts, watercress

SELENIUM

How It Affects The Body
- As an antioxidant, helps eliminate toxins from the body.
- A deficiency contributes to premature aging.

Good Food Sources

meat, seafood, cereals, broccoli, onions, tomatoes, tuna, asparagus, eggs, nuts, milk

ZINC

How It Affects The Body
- Promotes health of liver, bone and skin.
- Cleanses the blood of carbon dioxide.

Good Food Sources

liver, eggs, oysters, meats, milk, brewers yeast, whole grains, wheat bran, wheat germ, pumpkin seeds

There are more trace minerals than what are listed above, but not enough is known about them to mention here. The foods that contain these other minerals are included in the "Good Food Sources" listed above. If you eat those foods on a regular basis, chances are that you are getting all of the trace minerals you need.

Chapter 6

Controlling Body Fat

*M*ost of us fight an ongoing battle with fat; but for some, it's an all-out *war!* When trying to cut down on fat, we often take steps that appear to work in the beginning but only add to the problem in the long run. Our weight-control plan must become a way of life, or *it will never work.*

Let's clear up some misconceptions about weight loss before we progress. Personal change is difficult when we don't understand what we're supposed to do and why. Hopefully you'll profit from this information as much as I have.

First, make a distinction between the two types of fat—essential body fat and excess body fat. *Essential body fat* is necessary to maintain life and to reproduce. As mentioned before, men need at least 3 to 6 percent of their body weight to be essential fat, and women need 8 to 12 percent in order to maintain life. Essential fat is found in the heart, liver, lungs, bone marrow, intestines, spleen, kidneys, spinal cord, nerve tissue, brain and cell membranes. Women also carry essential body fat in mammary glands and the pelvic region, which accounts for the larger percentage.

Excess body fat, found in the tissue between muscle and skin, is basically fat that has been stored. We need some excess body fat to protect our bones and organs, to insulate our body from cold and heat and to maintain a good core body temperature. Average stored body fat is 12 to 15 percent of total body weight for men, and 15 to 25 percent for women. Problems occur when that figure rises above 20 percent for men and 30 percent for women.

Carrying too much fat in our bodies contributes to cardiovascular (heart) and pulmonary (lung) problems, high blood pressure, diabetes, gall bladder disease and cancer—not to mention fatigue and depression. Too much fat also stresses the metabolic system and creates more heat during physical activity due to having to move extra weight around. This makes it difficult to regulate body temperature when exercising. When body fat becomes *excessive,* heat can't move from the working muscles to the skin because of the layers of fat between them. As a result, heat exhaustion and heat stroke are a greater possibility.

You can also do as much damage to your health by letting your body weight fall too low as you do when you have too much fat. The body needs to be balanced. Complications of low body weight include disruption of the menstrual cycle (amenorrhea), anemia, slow heart rate, decreased cardiac output, low blood pressure and low white blood cell count. (More on that in Chapter 7.)

Body Weight vs. Body Fat

There is a difference in being overweight and being overfat. *Overweight* means the total body weight exceeds a standardized weight based on height and sex. A standarized weight table does not take into account bone structure and frame size, nor does it consider the relationship of lean muscle mass to stored body fat. You can be considered overweight by these tables even if you have low levels of body fat but higher weight in lean muscle and bone mass. Conversely, you can be *overfat* and yet still within the normal weight range for your height— because you have little muscle. Muscle is heavier than fat but has less bulk than the same weight in fat. For a healthy body, maintain a proper balance between muscle mass and fat.

Repeat after me: *The only healthy way to lose excess body fat is with a combination of proper diet and exercise.* (You may need to repeat that statement about fifty times, and have it etched on your mirror, branded into your wallet, embroidered on your favorite sweater or written on the palm of your hand.) Do whatever you have to do to get it into your brain and down to your soul. *To have healthy weight loss we must pay attention to both diet and exercise, not just one or the other.* Trying to lose weight by diet or exercise alone always results in frustration.

Physical inactivity increases storage fat and decreases muscle mass; it's an unchangeable law of physiology. Body fat increases as we age due to our sedentary lifestyles. Exercise can prevent that. But if you try to diet without exercise, you will end up losing lean body tissue as well.

Weight loss should be gradual. Any weight loss of more than two pounds a week means you are losing more than fat.

Desirable body weight has less to do with charts and fashion, and more to do with personal goals and attitudes toward body image. Aim for what is comfortable for you, and refuse to fall prey to the perfect-thin-body trap. Take into consideration genetics, your age and your health. We tend to beat ourselves up over a characteristic we've inherited (wide hips, thick ankles) instead of accepting it and changing things we can.

Using Fat as Fuel

The term *homeostasis* as it refers to the body indicates a state of equilibrium and stability of physiological function. In other words, the body easily does what it needs to do to continuously produce energy and remove wastes. It is internally balanced, not stressed, and the demands made upon it are easily met. Specifically, respiratory ventilation, cardiac output, blood flow and blood pressure all work without problems.

When we exercise, this state of equilibrium changes. If we exercise in sudden bursts of high intensity movement for short periods of time, we place stressful demands on the body's metabolic system, disrupting the homeostatic state.

Shop the Perimeters

By confining your shopping to the perimeters of a grocery store, you can avoid the maze of chemical-laden, sugared, salted, overprocessed temptation foods usually found in the center aisles. At times, you may cautiously venture into the center for healthy boxed cereals, natural fruit juice, popcorn or whole-grain items. But go in with a plan. Be focused on what you need and don't allow roaming eyes to lure you toward the dangers that lurk on every aisle.

On the other hand, less stressful movements that require a *moderate* amount of energy and are done over a longer period of time help establish a new level of homeostasis. This means that even when *not* exercising, your body will use energy and remove wastes at a higher metabolic rate. That's why it is important to establish a regular routine of moderate intensity aerobic exercise three to four times a week. You will begin to metabolize at a higher rate and burn calories even when you are resting.

Every cell in our body requires continuous energy. Food supplies that energy only indirectly. The immediately useable form of energy is ATP (adenosine triphosphate). Everything that happens in the body requires the breakdown of ATP.

Energy is produced when carbohydrates break down into glucose, which combines with oxygen to produce ATP. Some ATP is used immediately and a limited amount is stored for future use. Fat and protein also produce energy, but only in limited amounts.

ATP is stored in the most active cells, where it is needed most. However, since only a limited amount of ATP can be stored, it must be continually resynthesized. (This may seem complicated and technical, but it's really not. It's just that the terms are foreign to us. Understanding the physiology explained in the next few paragraphs can change your life. It changed mine.)

There are four ways ATP can be resynthesized. One way is the *phosphagen system*. You don't need to know any more about it other than that it provides energy for up to ten seconds of all-out effort. This is good for a sprint, a quick jog, pitching a ball or lifting something heavy.

The second way ATP is resynthesized is *anaerobic glycolysis*. *Anaerobic* means without the presence of oxygen, so ATP must be manufactured without oxygen. Anaerobic production of ATP is required when you need large bursts of energy over a period of one to three minutes. This is longer than the phosphagen system, which only provides energy for one to 10 *seconds*. Physical activity happens so quickly there isn't time for the cardiorespiratory system to supply oxygen to the working muscles. When this system breaks down glucose to ATP, lactic acid is the byproduct. If the circulatory system can't get rid of the lactic acid fast enough, it builds up and causes the muscle to fatigue and sometimes have a burning sensation. That is called lactic acid build-up.

The good part of anaerobic metabolism is that since oxygen is not needed, energy can be produced immediately. The bad news is that the energy is limited by how much lactic acid you can tolerate and still function. However, this system is good for developing muscular strength, such as lifting light weights, and toning specific muscles, such as the leg raises and abdominal curls. If you do these exercises at high intensity, you won't be able to go beyond one to three minutes.

The third way ATP is resynthesized for energy is the *aerobic metabolic pathway*. *Aerobic* means in the presence of oxygen, so this system requires a continual supply of oxygen to produce ATP. When oxygen is present, glucose is used to produce ATP. This process is only limited by the cardiorespiratory system's ability to deliver oxygen. It requires lower intensity exercise for a longer duration and is good for endurance activities of more than three and less than twenty minutes. By-products of this system are carbon dioxide (exhaled breath) and water (sweat), neither of which cause fatigue or pain. Aerobic exercise depends on the ability of the cardiovascular and respiratory systems to provide a continuous supply of oxygen to the working cells.

The fourth way ATP can be resynthesized is the method I'd most like you to pay attention to if you want to lose weight. It's called *fatty acid oxidation.* This is also aerobic, so it requires oxygen to produce ATP, but the exercise intensity is lower and the duration longer. After 20 minutes of this type of exercise, fat is burned as the primary source of fuel. Read this paragraph again, if you haven't already. This stuff is too good to go by without letting it sink in.

Do you realize what this means? It means that if you work a little *less hard* for a *little longer* time, you will burn fat! Anything you do after 20 minutes is pure fat burning. At least 20 minutes of exercise is needed to release fatty acid from the storage sites into the blood. There is a certain amount of fatty acid that will never be used as fuel unless low intensity exercise happens over a period of 20 minutes or longer.

Many of us break our backs doing 15 to 20 minutes of high-intensity exercise and wonder why we don't lose fat. The fuel source for high-intensity exercise is glucose; for low-intensity exercise over 20 minutes the fuel source is fat or fatty acid.

We can use any one of these systems any time we want. It's up to us—unless we are trying to keep from getting burned on the stove (phosphagen system), or are running from some threat of harm (anaerobic glycolysis), or trying to walk home from work before dark (aerobic metabolic pathway). In those situations, the circumstances dictate what system we will use. However, when it comes to exercise, *we* decide. The intensity, duration and type of movement we choose determines which metabolic system will predominate.

Easy Does It, You're Working Too Hard

Can you believe it? All this time we've killed ourselves trying to get fat off our bodies. We exercised as hard as we could, got sore and tired and when we didn't see results we got discouraged and depressed and gave up. In truth, we need to put in about 30 minutes worth of work, but we can do it at a more comfortable pace. It has to be within your target heart-rate zone, which is about 50 percent to 80 percent of your maximum heart rate. To make it simple, you should be able to sustain the pace for 30 minutes without respiratory distress and still work up a sweat about halfway through.

If during aerobic exercise you become winded or feel that you can't make it through the 20 to 30 minutes without stopping to rest, you are doing too much too fast. Pull back, take smaller steps, do smaller arm movements or eliminate arm movements altogether for the time being. The idea is to keep moving at a low to moderate rate for those 30 minutes in order to get oxygen into your blood and to all the working muscles, to burn fat and eliminate body waste.

If you are more than 30 pounds overweight, begin at 50 to 60 percent of your target heart rate. Rather than running or jumping, do only low-impact aerobics, cycling or walking. Be careful to avoid any movements that could injure your back, knees or ankles.

When you are exercising at low intensity, you may feel you're not working hard enough to make a difference. Don't let that fool you! What you are doing is establishing a new level of homeostasis for your system. In other words, your respiratory, cardiovascular and metabolic systems will rise to meet the body's new needs, and when you are *not* exercising it will work at a higher metabolic state. You will be burning calories even when resting. That is good news.

Understand that fat and muscle are separate entities; one cannot become the other. You increase fat and muscle differently. A scale, however, cannot distinguish one from the other and so the muscle and fat pounds read out the same. So when you exercise and build muscle, the scale may not show as much of a change as you might like. Don't worry about that. In fact, forget the scale for a few months. If you must measure something, measure inches lost, or jeans fitting more comfortably around the thighs, or jackets and dresses fitting more loosely under the arms, or skirts buttoning more easily at the waist.

People often mistakenly think they can get rid of dimpled fat (cellulite) with specific exercises for that area. The truth is only aerobic exercise for 20 to 30 minutes will burn off the fat. Those other kinds of exercises are anaerobic, and while they tone and firm the muscles being worked, they don't burn off fat.

Avoiding the Famine Syndrome

Remember, I said you have to eat right as well as exercise in order to have healthy weight loss. But many of us tend to go to extremes in the food department. Because we have misconceptions about what healthy weight loss is all about, we become involved in weight-loss programs that are neither balanced nor healthy. We focus only on losing fat instead of on preserving our health. We think that if cutting down on calories will help us lose a couple of pounds, then surely starving ourselves will do the job quickly and completely. *Wrong!*

Basically, healthy weight loss involves balancing calorie intake with calorie output. In other words, *body weight stabilizes at a healthy weight when caloric intake equals caloric expenditure.* An imbalance in those two causes the body to change weight. When you use more energy than is provided by the food you eat, your body draws on fat to supply what's missing. The billions of fat cells in our bodies don't disappear; they get smaller or larger depending on whether fat is burned or stored. When you eat more calories than you burn, you store what's left over as body fat.

Losing weight, then, requires two things: *reducing the number of calories you consume* as well as *increasing the number of calories you burn.* Doing one without the other gives you half a healthy body and half a healthy weight loss. Once again, *the best way to achieve a healthy weight loss is with a combination of diet and exercise.*

Don't aim to achieve the body ideal promoted by the fashion of the day. Instead, base your weight on what makes you feel your best. At what weight do you perform best? Do you have to be a size 10 or can you be happy in a size 12? I want to direct you away from unrealistic goals and practices that are not only ineffective but can be dangerous.

There *is* a way to achieve a desirable weight and maintain it. The first step is deciding that you want to change your lifestyle to benefit your health. *If the method you have adopted for losing weight is not one you can maintain for life, then it is imbalanced and may harm your body.* It surely will doom you to failure. Starvation or deprivation diets of any kind are extreme and should never be tried—not even once.

Fad diets attempt to make things easy for you, but they can never be a way of life, and as a result can never lead to permanent changes. Any severely restricted calorie intake is unnatural and there will *always* be a price to pay for it. Weight loss of more than two pounds per week is unhealthy, because besides fat you are losing lean body tissue as well. Lean body tissue is not only muscle, it's all other tissue in the body besides fat. That means you will be losing something from your skin, hair, fingernails, heart and blood vessels. None of us can afford to lose anything from those areas.

There is a theory that the body maintains a certain level of body fat for survival, depending on the conditions that are given it. That level is called *set point*. Eating healthy food and getting 30 minutes of aerobic exercise three to four times a week balances intake with output, and the body will stabilize at a comfortable weight and not be overfat. If, however, you go on a diet that is unbalanced, unnatural or extremely restricted and your weight quickly drops below your current set-point level, your body will think it's starving and immediately lower its metabolism to conserve energy. As a result, it will retain the fat you have to protect you from starvation.

A high-fat diet will increase your set point. A severely restricted diet will lower it. If you go back and forth, up and down, over and over, the set-point mechanism becomes inefficient. You will find that with each new crash diet, it becomes easier to gain weight and harder to lose it.

Quick-weight-loss diets usually cause loss of muscle, glycogen and water. Sometimes we think we are

Don't Forget About Your Honey

Far too many people have never developed an appreciation of the healthiest sweet-tooth satisfier—honey. What could be better than a piece of whole-grain toast or a bowl of fresh, hot oatmeal (not the quick-cook mush kind) with honey on top? It's the best. It's also guilt free. Honey contains potassium, chlorine, magnesium, silica, iron, copper, enzymes, amino acids and vitamins B and C. It also enhances the absorption of zinc and magnesium. It can even heal certain skin conditions. Sugar, by contrast, weakens bones by inhibiting calcium absorption in the intestines. To get the greatest benefit from honey, buy it raw and unprocessed.

losing fat when actually we are losing *health*. These kinds of diets lead to vitamin and mineral deficiencies, weakness, kidney problems, fatigue and nausea.

Frequent dieting and severe restriction of calories leads the body to get used to fewer calories. This means that eventually the same level of calorie intake that caused you to lose weight will cause you to maintain the same weight or even cause a weight gain. *Yo-yo dieting*, the up-and-down cycles of weight gain and loss, actually cause the body to resist losing weight. This is because the metabolic rate is lowered to protect the body against starvation. Losing lean body mass and increasing fat further lowers metabolism. This means you have to restrict calories even more in order to lose fat.

The good news is that our plan—30 minutes of aerobic exercise three to four times a week—*will* increase the body's metabolic rate, and as a result, lower the set point. It works like this: After you finish exercising aerobically, your metabolic rate stays elevated for hours, even when you are resting. This increases your energy output beyond what your effort is. Exercise helps you to increase the energy you expend and the fat you burn without losing any lean muscle mass. But it must be *aerobic* exercise that is of moderate intensity, sustained for over 20 minutes. Weight-lifting won't burn calories at the same rate as fast walking. Aerobic exercise helps you burn fat, develop better muscle tone and improve the efficiency of your cardiovascular system. The greater your aerobic capacity, the better your ability will be to use fat.

Getting organized

Trying to lose weight without *aerobic* exercise means you have a lot going against you. Aerobically fit persons have trained their bodies to get rid of fat continuously. Their body works for them round the clock. If you aren't aerobically fit, your body won't do that for you. The only time you *lose* fat is when you starve yourself, and that's not fair to your body. If you are cruelly and inconsiderately depriving your body of the aerobic exercise it needs, I want to give you an assignment. *STOP THAT!* Apologize to yourself, and commit to changing your ways.

Determine right now that there will be change and answer the following questions:
• What days can you do your 30 minutes of aerobics?

- What time of day will it be?
- Did you write these exercise times in your appointment book or calendar? Do that, so when you are asked to do something else at the same time you can check your book and say, "I'm sorry, I have an appointment."
- What activity are you going to do? Pick one or more of the following: fast walking, an aerobic class, a step class, an aerobic tape, stationary bike, treadmill or stair-step machine.
- Do you have properly supporting athletic shoes that feel so good you can hardly wait to get them on and exercise? If not, when can you buy a pair?
- Do you have loose-fitting, comfortable clothes to wear?

Your chances of succeeding increase dramatically if you are organized when it comes to exercising and eating right. This part of your life is too crucial to be left to chance. Make it a priority.

During the first few months of your aerobic exercise program, don't worry if you don't see much change on the scales. Lean weight is being built at about the same rate as fat is being lost. Don't let that worry you. You are still getting thinner and your clothes will be fitting more loosely.

What to Avoid

If you go on a particular diet to lose weight that cannot become a way of life, then it is not right for you. Don't fall victim to any of the following methods which can never provide a healthy, sustainable weight loss.

Fad diets of any kind that interfere with your intake of *nutrients* are dangerous. People assume they are losing fat but the fat is untouched. *Extreme low calorie diets* mean potassium and calcium depletion, dehydration and ketosis, or increased blood acids. *Unbalanced diets* that recommend eating one or two kinds of food for extended periods of time lead to vitamin and mineral deficiencies. These diets exact a heavy price and they do not encourage permanent change in eating habits.

101

If the method

you have

adopted for

losing weight

is not one

you can

maintain

for life,

then it is

imbalanced

and may harm

your body.

They lead people to believe that they can lose weight quickly with little effort, a concept that is not accurate.

Following rigid rules without learning to make good nutritional choices will never have the long-term results you desire. As soon as you stop living rigidly, the weight comes back.

Severe caloric restriction results in losing large amounts of water, minerals, glycogen, electrolytes and protein, but very little fat. Instead, cut down a little from what you normally eat, add more fresh vegetables and fruits, and combine it with moderate aerobic exercise. I guarantee you will see a moderate weight loss without harming your body. And you can sustain this as a way of life.

The American College of Sports Medicine recommends that you cut down no more than 500 calories at a time until you adjust to that.

Get rid of calories by reducing fat and sugar intake, and eating fewer foods that are devitalized of nutrients. Eat slowly, chewing every bite well—*and do not take second helpings*. Keeping records of all the foods you eat for two or three weeks will give you an idea of where to cut back. Eat low-fat, high-nutrient foods instead.

You must eat well. If your body is not properly fed, you cannot exercise. If you can't exercise, you cannot burn fat. If you don't eat well you won't have high enough levels of hemoglobin, which comprise the molecules in red blood cells that carry oxygen. If you can't carry oxygen in your blood, the cells in your body die.

Plastic or rubber suits worn to melt fat away while exercising are ineffective, since it is water that is lost, not fat. These suits are dangerous because perspiration cannot evaporate, which plays havoc with your ability to regulate body temperature during exercise. This could lead to dehydration, heat cramps and possibly heat stroke.

Diet pills contain stimulants like amphetamines, and temporarily curb your appetite. But you can become addicted to them and end up with high blood pressure, headaches, irregular heart rhythm, liver damage and insomnia—and still not achieve permanent weight loss.

Liposuction is a method of vacuuming fat cells out of the body. This is not a way to lose weight. In fact, doctors who perform these operations usually won't do so if the person is more than 40 pounds overweight. The surgery is used mainly for cosmetic purposes, on people who are at a good weight, but still can't get rid of fat pockets despite low-fat diets combined with aerobic exercise. The common areas of such fat pockets are thighs, the abdomen, knees, hips and under the chin.

Intestinal bypass, gastric stapling and the *gastric bubble* can all have serious and often life-threatening complications. I understand why in desperation some people resort to these methods. I do not condemn anyone for it. In fact, I wish I *could* recommend a weight-loss method that would work quickly and easily, with no side-effects, but I can't, because there isn't one.

When we lose weight too quickly, there is always a steep price to pay. The payment is taken out of your health. The method I recommend may take longer, but you will be rewarded with a longer and healthier life. Nothing else works but a change of habits and lifestyle.

Sugar also should be avoided. I repeat my earlier warning: sugar does not improve your ability to exercise, and in fact may impair it. When you eat sugar, it enters the bloodstream and raises the blood-sugar level. The body reacts to this by producing insulin, which lowers the blood sugar level but inhibits fatty acid metabolism. Consequently, muscles rely on glycogen instead of fat for energy. That's why *it is impossible get rid of fat when there is sugar in the body.* As the muscles draw on glycogen, the blood-sugar level falls, making you weak and exhausted.

Caffeine, found in coffee, tea, colas, chocolate and aspirin, stimulates the central nervous system. It is a diuretic and can contribute to dehydration through water loss if you don't drink enough water when you are sweating profusely. Ingesting too much caffeine leads to headache, nausea and muscle tremors.

Salt is found in sufficient quantities in our diet. Any extra salt draws water out of the cells and contributes to dehydration. That's why it's best to replace fluid lost in sweat with plain water.

Alcohol is something we should avoid, but especially before exercising. It directs blood flow away from the heart to the surface of the skin and depresses the central nervous system, interfering with balance and coordination. Drinking and exercise increases the risk of serious accident, heart problems, and contributes to weight gain.

Junk food must become taboo for you. Learn to see candy, cake, pie, soft drinks, chips and highly-processed food as part of the death process. These things should never be a part of your life, other than for occasional celebrations. If you feel you can't live without it, pick the junk food you love most and restrict yourself to eating it only *once* a *week* at *one sitting*. Better yet, find a substitute you can enjoy.

A friend who can't live without ice cream found a substitute in a health food store that is made with healthy ingredients and is not fattening. After a few weeks of substituting it, her taste buds have changed and she enjoys it as much as ice cream—*without* the guilt. You can train taste buds to like anything, but you can't keep torturing and tempting them with foods they shouldn't have. Avoid those foods altogether—your taste buds will get over it eventually.

Low-Fat Choices in a High-Fat World

Cutting down on fat intake is the focus of our day. The reason for that is our predominantly high-fat diet, combined with our knowledge that excess fat increases the risk of heart disease, high cholesterol, high blood pressure and breast, colon and prostate cancers. The recommended percentages of fat intake are decreasing, and what is suggested today will probably be considered high by next year. The point is to cut down on fat and to make low-fat choices whenever possible. This will improve your chances for a longer, healthier life. Remember that everything you do counts. It all adds up—for bad or for good. Fat is no exception.

I recommend that you purchase a pocket-sized book showing grams of fat in every food, and use it as a reference. But don't worry about which fruit or vegetable has the most fat. They all have so many vitamins and minerals that eliminating some of them could possibly shut out your only source of that nutrient. With the exception of avocados (which also contain important vitamins and minerals), vegetables and fruits contain such a small amount of fat in comparison to other foods that it's not worth eliminating them from your diet. It's better to cut out fat in other areas. Too much fat in a diet *never* comes from too many fruits and vegetables! Eat them in peace. Instead, watch high-fat meats, dairy products, cakes, cookies, chips, processed foods and fried foods.

Here's how to keep a close watch on the fat content of your food and help you to determine what percentage of your diet is fat. You can also use this formula to determine what percentage of a particular food is fat when fat grams are listed on the label. Remember, a low-calorie product can be high in fat.

The formula is as follows:

Step 1: Total the number of calories you are eating (in a day, in a meal, in one particular food).

Step 2: Total the number of fat grams you are eating. (Found on a fat-gram chart or a label.)

Step 3: Multiply the grams of fat by 9, the number of calories in a gram of fat. (There are 4 calories in a gram of protein and 4 calories in a gram of carbohydrate.)

Step 4: Divide the total (of the grams of fat times 9) by the number of calories you are eating.

For example, if I ate 2000 calories today and 100 grams of those were from fat, I would multiply 100 x 9 to get 900 calories from fat. I would then divide the 900 calories by 2000 calories and I would find that 45% of my calories came from fat. This is way too high and I would need to cut down.

You don't have to drive yourself crazy with this. Just be aware, be wise and make healthy low-fat choices whenever possible. Try to eat *healthy* while at the same time cutting down on fat.

Point Me in the Right Direction

Many people ask me for a sample week's menu and health activities, to get them started right. Below is a skeleton schedule to help get you organized. But ultimately you must create a schedule that will work for *you* to get a variety of foods in your diet, consider what is available in your area and the season you're in. If possible, seek the advice of a professional who can examine you and determine your past habits and present needs. Until you find such a person, here is a typical day's worth of suggestions. Adjust them to fit your needs:

6:00 a.m.
- Wake up and say, "Thank you God for this wonderful day"—or some other expression of thanksgiving and praise.
- Go to the kitchen and get 16 ounces (2 cups) of fresh pure water. Buy the best bottled water you can get if your water is not pure or doesn't taste good. Squeeze the juice of half a lemon into it (save the other half for later).
- As you are drinking your water, read a chapter of the Bible and pray to God about everything that concerns you this day.
- Decide at this time when you will exercise and for how long. Will it be before breakfast, before lunch, before dinner or before bedtime? Write it into your schedule.
- Get ready for the day. (Exercise, shower, get dressed, etc.)

7:00 a.m.
- Prepare a whole-grain cereal. While it's cooking, eat one to three pieces of fresh fruit from the Fruit Chart (Chart A). For example, one papaya, or an

apple. Or a cantaloupe. Or an orange. Or one cup
of fresh strawberries. Get a good variety throughout the week. Do not use canned, frozen or cooked
fruit unless fresh is not available. Eat slowly and
give your body time to break it down and absorb it.
Then eat the whole grain cereal. Either put honey
on it, or a banana chopped up, or non-fat milk.

8:30–10:30 a.m.

- If you haven't yet exercised, do it now.

10:30–11:00 a.m.

- Drink 16 ounces of water with the other half of the
lemon squeezed into it. If you are going to exercise
between 10:00 and 12:00, drink the water first.

12:00 p.m.

- Have lunch. Choose vegetables from the Vegetable
Chart (Chart A). Eat them raw, in a salad, lightly
steamed or baked, or in a soup. Have a grain like
sprouted bread, whole grain pasta or whole grain
crackers with it. Or have a light protein, such as
tuna or turkey breast.

2:00–3:00 p.m.

- Exercise, if you haven't done so already.

3:00–4:00 p.m.

- Drink 16 ounces of fresh pure water with juice from
half a lime squeezed into it.

4:30 p.m.

- Have an afternoon snack, if you're hungry. A
handful of grapes, an apple, or a banana with a
few nuts (almonds), or seeds (sunflower), low-fat
plain yogurt with blueberries, etc.

6:00 p.m.

- Have dinner. This should include a protein and at
least two vegetables. You can include a whole grain
at this time also. Eat as much of the vegetables as
you wish. The protein and grain will fill you up the
rest of the way. You should not leave the table
hungry.

107

8:00–9:00 p.m.
- Drink 16 ounces of pure fresh water with the juice of half a lime in it.

8:00–9:00 p.m.
- Exercise, if you haven't already done so, and if it won't keep you awake later. If you need a snack after exercising, try raw fruit or a vegetable.

10:00 p.m.
- Bedtime

I have provided a simple Quick Checklist (Chart B) to help keep you organized. Make enough copies for 21 days—to get you used to the routine. If you are out and about during the day, take your water with you. Buy small bottles of water for that purpose or take a thermos of water from home. It's not such a big thing, so don't look at it as a chore. It's something to make a part of your life and you just do it.

Make yourself cultivate a love for vegetables and fruits. They are a vital part of your life so get the freshest and tastiest available. Pay attention to what's in season and ask your grocer about the most recent delivery or most highly recommended produce.

Always look for ways to cut fat out of what you're eating, and make healthier substitutions.

Check out these charts!

Fruits

apples	mango
apricots	oranges
bananas	papaya
blackberries	peaches
blueberries	pears
boysenberries	pineapple
cantaloupes	plums
cherries	prunes
grapefruit	raspberries
grapes	strawberries
guava	tangerines
kiwis	watermelon

Vegetables

avocado	lima beans
beet tops	okra
beets	onion
broccoli	parsley
brussels sprouts	peas
cabbage	red potatoes
carrots	red peppers
cauliflower	russet potatoes
celery	spinach
chard	squash
corn	sweet potatoes
cucumbers	tomatoes
eggplant	turnips
green peppers	white potatoes
lentils	yellow peppers
lettuce	zucchini

Chart B

You have permission to photocopy this page for daily use.

Quick Checklist

_____ I drank sixteen ounces of water when I woke up.

_____ I prayed and read the Bible.

_____ I determined to exercise at one of the following times:

　　_____ Before breakfast　　TIME _____

　　_____ Between breakfast and lunch

　　　　　　　　　　　TIME _____

　　_____ Between lunch and dinner

　　　　　　　　　　　TIME _____

　　_____ Between dinner and bedtime

　　　　　　　　　　　TIME _____

_____ I ate fresh fruit for breakfast.

TYPE _____

_____ I ate whole grains for breakfast.

TYPE _____

_____ I also ate: _____

_____

_____ I drank sixteen ounces of water at least one hour before lunch.

_____ For lunch I ate at least 50% raw or lightly cooked fresh vegetables.

TYPE _____

_____ I also ate: _____

_____

_____ I drank sixteen ounces of water at least one hour before dinner.

_____ For dinner I ate:

　　　　50% vegetables　TYPE _____

　　　　Protein　　　　　TYPE _____

_____ I also ate: _____

_____

What were my sources of calcium today?

_____

_____ I drank sixteen ounces of water at least an hour after dinner.

_____ I went to bed in time to get eight hours of sleep.

Chapter 7

Why We Struggle

We eat to sustain life. We also eat because we enjoy it and it is an important part of celebration. But food was never meant to be a reward, an object of obsessive focus or a substitute for love and acceptance. Yet for many of us, eating has become something more than it was intended to be. Most of us occasionally eat foods that are bad for us, or overeat foods that taste good. But I'm talking about destructive, out-of-control eating patterns that can ruin our health.

Sometimes we do the wrong things because we don't understand the *right* things to do—or we don't understand *why* we need to do them. But besides a lack of knowledge about proper exercise and good food choices, there are several other reasons our eating can get out of control. See if any of these apply to you.

The Depleted Body

One reason we overeat, eat compulsively or eat the wrong things is that our bodies are *depleted*. We lack something, and eat to try to make up for it. Our bodies can be depleted by stress, trauma, overwork, eating nutritionally

The Exhausted Perfectionist

If you start each day with a long list of things you think you should be, do and feel, you could be defeating your purpose. Having to look perfect, act perfect and feel perfect all the time is exhausting. It's far more productive to list things we know we can't do and give them to God, along with thanks for his strength to do what is necessary. Refuse to let the pressure you put on yourself take life away from you. Instead, turn to the Source of Life and cast your cares on him, knowing he is all the perfection you need.

depleted food, illness, taking drugs, drinking alcohol, serious injury, numerous surgeries and pregnancy—especially multiple pregnancies in close succession. Another simple reason that we often overlook is a lack of rest.

If you don't get enough rest every night, your body will become depleted. When you are overtired *and* depleted, you may find yourself hungry all the time, or needing to eat to make you feel better. What you need more than food at a time like that is deep, sound sleep.

A lack of rest can start a cycle of overeating or eating poorly, which causes you to not sleep well when you do find time to rest. This makes you *more* depleted and leads to more wrong food choices. Now you're too tired to exercise, so you can't get rid of the waste products in your body. This causes more fatigue and keeps you from being able to sleep well, which causes you to eat more to make up for how lousy you feel. *STOP!* If you recognize yourself in this description, go to bed and get some rest.

In order to do that, shut off your mind to your problems, lower the volume on your phone, turn off the T.V., put down your book, stick ear plugs in your ears, drape the windows so light doesn't come in, inform your friends that you need to rest and ask that they not drop over or call after a certain hour. Then read a few Psalms, get into your most comfortable jammies, and snuggle in. Do this an hour or two earlier than usual every night for three weeks, and you'll feel like a new person. Getting more rest even for a few nights may allow you to feel like exercising, which will also help you to sleep better at night. Sleeping and exercising will give you the strength to make calm, sane, unpressured food choices, because you won't be eating to try to make up for how terribly exhausted, depleted and empty you feel. Sometimes you can feel like you're starving when actually you have eaten plenty. Exercise and sleep help the hunger pangs subside. It's amazing how that works.

You may be saying, "But you don't know my schedule. I can't get to bed any earlier. I've got too much to do." I understand being overloaded, but I've learned that if we are too busy to get rest, then we are *too busy*! Something has to give before your body does. My advice is to *make rest a priority*.

Ask for help. Learn to delegate responsibility. Say no. Make better use of the time you have. God never asks us to give beyond what we have. You are only one person, who has only 24 hours in your day, and your life has to work within those parameters. If you are not able to give your body enough rest, then your life is not working. Check to see where you can make some changes.

Lack of rest could be the cause of problems with your eating.

Feeding Rejection

Sometimes we need to lose *emotional* baggage before we can start losing weight. Most people who struggle with their weight really desire good health, but can't bring their actions into alignment with their heart. They eat uncontrollably, then feel guilty about it, not to mention the discomfort of lugging around extra weight on a skeletal frame never designed to carry it.

Is willpower the problem? Partly, but there is more to it than that. Do they really want to exercise and eat right? I believe they do. But there is something in the deepest part of their being that works against their desires. The warfare is exhausting, defeating and seemingly hopeless. It seems easier to forget the whole thing and eat.

There are many theories about why people struggle with their weight or have eating disorders, but no one seems to have all the answers. After years of talking with these strugglers and listening as they reveal their personal lives to me, I've found they all have something in common: each struggles with long-standing rejection. Either they have been rejected numerous times, or they have experienced at least one traumatic rejection that dogged them the rest of their lives. Some could not recall any specific instances of rejection, but admitted that they felt rejected nonetheless. One possible reason for those feelings is having a parent who didn't want them. Children pick up those messages even though they aren't verbalized. In any case, *feelings* of rejection are real, whether or not specific incidents of it can be recalled.

All of us have been rejected at one time or another, whether by family members, friends, teachers, casual acquaintances or even strangers. When we're emotionally healthy, rejection doesn't set us back permanently. We are soon able to gain perspective and brush it off, because we know who we are and that we have worth. But if we have emotional scars from even one traumatic incident of rejection, a relatively insignificant word, look or action can plunge a knife of rejection deep into our hearts.

Recovery from rejection happens when we learn to see ourselves as God sees us. We must understand that *God* does not reject us, and he says we don't have to live with feelings of rejection.

I once heard a gifted pastor named Jerry Cook describe how God sees us. He said, "God views us through our future. We view ourselves from our past." We look at our failures and the way we are at this moment. God looks at us the way he made us to be. He sees the end result. You may have been rejected all of your life, even by a parent, but realize that God accepts you as you are—because he sees your future. Learn to stop looking at your past and see your future through God's eyes.

When you are tormented by rejection, you come to believe that you are unworthy of acceptance and begin to expect rejection. Then, you interpret the words and actions of others through the eyes and ears of rejection. *Rejection must be fed.* You expect it. You see it. You hear it. You feel it.

The more we hear "I'm *not* acceptable, I *am* rejectable" in our minds, the more we feed our feelings of rejection, until they begin to control us. Then, rejection lives in us; it's always there, even when we try to resist it.

Because rejection needs to be fed, there appears to be a connection between that emotional/spiritual malady and uncontrollable feeding of the body. Not everyone who overeats suffers from rejection, nor does everyone who struggles with rejection overeat. But a significant percentage of people with eating disorders and serious weight problems *do* suffer from feelings of rejection.

Do you ever feel rejected? If so, at those times when you feel badly about yourself, is food a comfort to you? If it is, then find out why. It could turn your whole life around.

Don't let someone's words or actions or an unhappy memory start a red light of rejection flashing in your brain. That red light indicates that your future has been clouded by your past. Don't let that happen.

Refuse to accept feelings of rejection, no matter how tempted you are to agree with them. Say to yourself, "God accepts and loves me the way I am. Therefore, I refuse to live in the pain of rejection any longer." Many of us live every day with feelings of rejection. Make sure *you're* not living with them—even mild forms. They may be a big part of the weight you carry around.

Anorexia Nervosa

Anorexia is an eating disorder based on a fear of fat. It usually occurs in adolescence to early twenties, and most commonly affects middle- to upper-class Caucasian women who tend to be perfectionists. Only about 10 percent of those suffering from eating disorders are men, and many of those men are athletes whose weight is a matter of great concern.

Our society puts far too much pressure on women to be perfect. We are expected to be physically fit, attractive, energetic, organized, emotionally stable, creative and productive—all while keeping a spotless home, having model children, being a gourmet cook, keeping our husbands enraptured with our marital abilities. And don't forget that we should be enthusiastic and articulate conversationalists who love to listen to everyone's problems and meet everyone's needs anytime of the day or night....

I'm exhausted just talking about it! No one can do it all. Our bodies, minds and emotions weren't designed for such stress, and we can't carry it off for very long. When a young woman puts that degree of expectation upon herself, anorexia may be the result.

Typically, anorexics come from families where the father is gone a lot, is often busy or is emotionally distant. The girl has such a highly-connected relationship with her mother that she feels pressure to be a model child. She is so influenced by her mother that she doesn't feel free to make her own choices and develop her own identity. She tends to be an excellent student and often puts pressure on herself even when her parents don't. Anorexia usually is triggered by a traumatic event, such as the death of a loved one, physical or sexual abuse, or even being made fun of because of weight.

The anorexic feels she has no control over her life and the only way to take control is by refusing to eat. She usually is a compliant child who is an overachiever and a perfectionist. Nothing is ever good enough because she can never achieve perfection. As a result, she has low self-esteem no matter how attractive or capable she is.

One of the main symptoms of anorexia is a confused and distorted body image. Anorexics see themselves as fat no matter how thin they get. They refuse to maintain even minimal normal weight for their height and age. As a result of their extreme weight-loss, the menstrual cycle stops, as body fat drops below 10 percent.

Anorexics constantly deny they're hungry, but loss of appetite normally doesn't occur until the advanced stages. Also in later stages, they develop facial and body hair, but have less hair on their head. They have dry scalp and emaciated bodies due to the absence of fat below the skin, which makes them sensitive to cold. They also can have difficulty sitting because there is no fat to cushion the bones, and they suffer from joint pain. They are emotional and moody and can become obsessive about counting calories and restricting fats. They are compulsive exercisers. They say they're not hungry, but they drink a lot of water to fill themselves up. They secretly throw their food away. When they do eat, they pick at their food, they crave spices, and they may eat very slowly, cutting food into small pieces. They put themselves on such extremely rigid eating and exercising schedules that, as the disease progresses, they don't have time to socialize, and so become isolated.

Anorexics suffer from a lack of calcium, which leads to thinning of bones and osteoporosis, and nutritional deficiencies, which lead to infections and disease. Eventually, the body has difficulty digesting, absorbing and metabolizing food, which leads to constipation, anemia, wasting away of the gastrointestinal tract, decreased muscle mass, abdominal pain, sleep disorder and hormonal imbalance. Mental confusion happens as a result of these deficiencies and imbalances.

As cells are destroyed, an electrolyte imbalance occurs, causing cardiac irregularities. This is the most serious symptom. When there is extreme calorie restriction and no fat, the muscles are broken down and used for energy. The body eats itself in order to survive. The heart, a muscle, decreases in size. The heart rate slows, blood pressure lowers and a heart attack can occur. Anorexia is a heart problem in *every* sense of the word.

If you or someone close to you shows a number of these symptoms, get yourself or them to a doctor immediately. Because anorexia is life-threatening, anorexics need professional help. See a medical doctor for advice on treatment. Don't treat this as if it's a school girl's harmless whimsy. It is a serious threat to life and should always be viewed as such. I've known people who said about their anorexic daughters, "She's fine now because she's eating and has gained her weight back," only to have her suddenly take a turn for the worse and, in some cases, die. Statistics show that seven percent of anorexics die of the complications of anorexia. Even weight gain does not always indicate a cure. During times of stress or when life is overwhelming, anorexics return to self-imposed starvation, and they can do it without alerting those close to them. Don't let that happen to you or someone you know.

Anorexics believe lies about themselves and those lies have to be exposed before they destroy the person. Their worth has to be firmly established in their heart. They have to be able to forgive not only others, but also themselves for not being perfect, for failing to be what they think they should be. They have to be convinced that they have worth apart from anyone or anything. They have to know that the thinnest people are not the happiest people, and worth has nothing to do with weight or appearance.

Symptoms of Anorexia

Chart A

- fear of fat
- loss of appetite
- extreme weight loss
- loss of hair
- irregular, or cessation of, menstrual periods
- frequently saying, "I'm not hungry"
- depression and concern over physical appearance
- a drive for perfection
- feelings of guilt
- feelings that who she is and what she does are not good enough
- feelings of not being able to live up to certain standards, either real or self-imposed
- lack of understanding about the seriousness of the problem

Bulimia

In contrast to anorexia, bulimia is a binge-purge cycle in which large amounts of food are eaten in a short time and then vomited. Additionally, bulimics control weight with laxatives, excessive exercise, diuretics and fasting. A preoccupation with body image and weight leads them to become obsessed with food. During binges, their eating is completely out of control. Anorexics suffer severe weight loss, while bulimics may have frequent fluctuations in their weight.

Bulimia is also most common in women from teenage to mid-twenties. College women are the highest risk group, while under five percent of men become bulimic. Bulimics understand that their eating disorder is a problem and are often depressed about it. Anorexics consider their eating disorder to be normal and a source of pride. Bulimics are frequently hungry, anorexics deny being hungry. Bulimics are not usually good students, anorexics are perfectionists. Bulimics look fine, anorexics look emaciated. Bulimics are aware of counting calories, anorexics are obsessed with it. Bulimics drink liquid to be able to vomit. Anorexics drink liquid to feel full and not gain weight. Bulimics eat fast and gulp their food down. Anorexics eat slowly and chew their food carefully.

Bulimics carefully plan meals, where they will eat and where they will vomit. The pleasure of eating this way comes not from the taste of the food so much as in avoiding the problem that triggered the binge. The vomiting is pleasurable because of the release it brings. Bulimics usually have dysfunction in their families and, as a result, have low self-esteem, depression and suicidal feelings. Both bulimics and anorexics try to control their bodies. Both set their goals too high and fall into despair when they can't attain them.

Other indications of bulimia are gastrointestinal disorders, tooth damage, chronic sore throat, difficulty in swallowing, electrolyte imbalance and rupture of the esophagus. Dehydration results from vomiting, as well as the use of laxatives and diuretics. The diuretics get rid of water weight, which returns immediately. Laxatives work only in the large intestine, and so are ineffective in preventing the absorption of calories, a small intestine function. Continued use of laxatives renders the colon unable to function normally.

Bulimics can suffer heart failure also, but not because the heart muscle has deteriorated as with anorexics. It happens when they suddenly stop habitual vomiting. This causes a particular chemical imbalance which leads to irregular heart beat and possible heart failure.

Like anorexia, bulimia requires professional help. Changing this behavior is too big an undertaking to handle alone. The earlier help is sought, the better will be the results. Suspect an eating disorder if someone complains of being fat when clearly her body is not even close to that, when she exercises excessively, when her weight goes up and down in short periods of time, if her hands, face and ankles bloat—also if she has muscle cramps, fatigue, frequent dental problems and she talks about diet pills, laxatives and diuretics. If you see any of these symptoms get help for her.

Eating disorders are a no-win situation. Anyone who suffers from them will wind up the loser. There is a wonderful life apart from food obsession. Do whatever is necessary to find it.

Symptoms of Bulimia

Chart B

- obsession with food
- out-of-control eating followed by vomiting
- frequent fluctuation in weight
- irregular heartbeat
- exercises obsessively
- muscle cramps, fatigue and light-headedness
- frequent dental problems
- constantly hungry
- eats fast and gulps the food down
- bloating of the hands, face and ankles
- takes large quantities of laxatives, diet pills or diuretics
- complains about being fat when they clearly are not

Learning Not To Be Hard On Yourself

If you do everything you know to do and still make self-destructive choices, seek the help of a counselor or doctor who specializes in eating disorders. Don't try to do it alone if doing that is not working. And don't be discouraged about it, because you can definitely be helped. Your problems are deep-rooted and you need others to help you identify them and sort them out. They can also help you handle the negative emotions that are keeping you from doing what's right for yourself. Don't stop searching until you have found the key.

Although most of us don't succumb to eating disorders, we do struggle year after year, losing weight then gaining it back. Weary from the struggle, we feel defeated, frustrated and guilty. If you've experienced that discouraging cycle, you may need a strong support system to help you eat right and exercise. Plant yourself in a good solid support group where you feel loved, accepted and comfortable, and where you can freely share feelings and concerns. Godly, praying relationships where you can bare your soul and be prayed for are best. Ask God to help you find people like that. It can mean the difference between success and failure.

Don't get hung up on pounds, calories, scales, fashion magazines and television commercials. *Be good to yourself.* Concentrate instead on health, energy, well-being and a zest for life. Don't put yourself in the *all-or-nothing* box: "Either I lose all this weight and fit into these jeans in four weeks or forget it!" Nobody can meet those requirements. Don't say, "I ate a cookie, now I might as well eat whatever I want because I've failed so miserably." Eating a cookie means nothing more than you ate a cookie. Don't make it into a bigger deal than that. It does not mean "I ate a cookie, therefore I'm fat, I'm ugly, I'm a failure, I can't do anything right, I'll be sick, I'm going to weigh a thousand pounds, why live, I might as well be dead...." That, my friend, is covering up your future with your past. Don't allow it.

Instead, stand up and say, "Success and happiness do not depend on inches and pounds, but rather on knowing I was created for a high purpose, which has *absolutely nothing* to do with what I look like or what I weigh."

That is the truth—and the truth always sets us free!

Don't get hung up on pounds, calories, scales, fashion magazines and television commercials. Concentrate instead on health, energy, well-being and a zest for life.

Chapter 8

The Healing Aspect of Food and Exercise

The older we get, the more important it becomes to take measures to ensure we have:

- health
- energy
- strength
- endurance
- good balance
- flexibility
- and an optimistic attitude about life.

Along with proper exercise and a healthy diet, what will most help us achieve these things is a close and loving relationship with God. A right combination of all three can prevent or improve many of the diseases that make life miserable as we grow older.

Let's look at some of the conditions that can be prevented or helped by proper diet and exercise. Perhaps you don't suffer from these problems now, but you could someday. So take a few precautionary steps to prevent—or at least delay—these disorders.

Heart Disease and High Cholesterol

Coronary disease is caused by *atherosclerosis*, the buildup of fatty deposits in the walls of the arteries. As the arteries become harder and the passages narrower, blood flow decreases. When that happens, a clot can easily develop and stop blood flow completely. If the clog plugs the artery to the heart, a *heart attack* results. If it plugs the artery to the brain, it causes a *stroke*.

The main culprit in all this is *cholesterol*, which is fat in the blood. Eating food high in *saturated fat* leads to high cholesterol and clogged arteries. As I mentioned earlier, the bad cholesterol (LDLs or low-density lipo-proteins) carries cholesterol into the system. Good cholesterol (HDLs, or high-density lipo-proteins) removes fatty deposits from the system through the liver.

A healthy, balanced, low-fat diet and aerobic exercise strengthen your heart, lower your cholesterol *and* help prevent heart disease. Choose brisk walking, aerobic classes, swimming, bicycling or stair-stepping, but be sure to do some activity regularly. It doesn't have to be a major effort. In fact, just being more active during leisure time can make a difference in your life. Instead of watching T.V., turn it off and go for a walk. If you can't do that, exercise while you watch T.V.

Too many people suffer and die from preventable heart disease and high cholesterol.

Osteoporosis

Osteoporosis is a condition where bones lose substance and become weak and brittle. As bone mass decreases, there is an increased likelihood of fractures. Because of their small bone mass as well as a decrease in estrogen after menopause, older women are more susceptible to osteoporosis. Also more likely to suffer from osteoporosis are Caucasian or oriental women who are small-boned and thin. Other risk factors include smoking, high alcohol and caffeine consumption, low calcium intake and a sedentary lifestyle. Drinking too many soft drinks raises your risk because a high intake of phosphorous increases the need for calcium.

According to the American Council on Exercise, the bone mass a woman has by age 35 affects how susceptible she is to fractures later on. That's because the body builds most of its bone by that age. Thinning of the bones as we get older is not inevitable; weight-bearing exercise can make a difference. In weight-bearing exercise, the bones bear the weight of the body. When bones are stressed by extra weight, they react like muscles and become stronger. Calcium is deposited in your bones as you exercise, making them stronger and more dense. Now is the time to start weight-bearing exercise because the thicker your bones are today, the stronger they will be later on. It's motivating to think of weight-bearing exercise depositing calcium in your bones. *It's an investment in your future!*

The problem for some of us is that we don't see our bones as living, growing tissue. Instead, we think of them as hard, rock-like structures, basically unchanging except for slight erosion that occurs over a lifetime. But in reality, bones respond immediately to weight-bearing movement and muscle contractions. Calcium is deposited into them to strengthen them to bear the weight. Just as muscles develop when they are used, so do bones.

People who lead sedentary lives are more susceptible to osteoporosis later in life. Those of us over 35 should be engaged in some form of weight-bearing exercise every day. Even if you do aerobics three times a week, be sure to include some weight-bearing activity on the other days. An active daily life, along with walking, running, stair climbing and light weight lifting, is sufficient.

Start today to build your bone mass. Eating right and exercising regularly *can* help prevent bone loss and osteoporosis.

Arthritis

People with arthritis once were advised to rest and avoid exercise. Now we know it's better to do the exact opposite. Rest can make arthritis pain worse, because joints stiffen with lack of use. Arthritis is a degeneration of the joint structures that gets worse with time and causes severe pain with movement. It tends to occur in areas of the body that have been injured. Although arthritis sufferers should avoid high-impact

There is a danger in trying to be so emotionally perfect that we don't allow ourselves a good gut-level, sobbing cry when we need it. A healing release occurs when we audibly cry out from the depths of our being, not settling for a misty-eyed, blinking-back-the-tears, lump-in-our-throat kind of emotion. I'm convinced there would be less depression and anger, and fewer health problems and headaches, if we would allow ourselves time and space to cry, out loud, when we need to.

moves, moderate exercise that maintains flexibility and strength can help. Walking, bicycling, swimming and moderate intensity, low-impact aerobic exercises also are beneficial. People with arthritis so severe they lose full use of their hands or feet have seen great improvement with a healthy diet and proper exercise. No matter how old you are, you can benefit.

A joint, where two bones meet, is covered with cartilage and surrounded by a capsule called the *synovium*. The capsule contains synovial fluid, which is vital to the joint mobility. When you exercise, synovial fluid is produced and spread over the joint, increasing circulation to the area. This lubricates, feeds and cleanses the tissues, which reduces swelling, removes waste products and helps to get oxygen and nutrients to the area. Besides making the bones stronger, exercise conditions and strengthens the muscles and ligaments *around* the bones, easing the pressure on the joints.

If you suffer from arthritis, exercises that increase your endurance, strength and flexibility will alleviate stiffness without jarring the joints. Exercise for flexibility every day, lift light weights every other day and take aerobic classes, swim, bicycle or walk.

As with all health concerns—when in doubt, have a doctor examine you and prescribe what is appropriate.

Stress

Our bodies were made to combat stress with exercise. When we face a tense situation, our bodies naturally prepare for physical action. However, we usually don't run from our foes or fight them, we try to stay calm and work it out. But the tension in our bodies, the stress hormones that are secreted, the constricted circulation that comes with stress, still need to be released somehow. The best method is exercise.

All stress, whether major or minor, adds up in the body. When you are stressed-out, eating right and exercising can make a difference in your ability to diffuse and cope with it. Exercise relaxes the muscles, especially if the activity is enjoyable, and neutralizes the negative effects of stress. It causes you to breathe deeper and take in more oxygen. It eliminates stress hormones and restores the levels of *norepinephrine*, an emotion-stabilizing hormone that is depleted by stress. It also causes you to sweat, which eliminates poisons in the body that add to your stress level. Regular aerobic exercise can place you ahead of the game and make you better able to withstand a stress-producing incident when it happens.

High Blood Pressure

Every time your heart beats, it sends blood through the body. The force it exerts against the walls of the arteries is called *systolic* pressure. Normal blood pressure is 120 over 80. Anyone who has a systolic measurement (that's the number at the top, or the first number mentioned) of more than 140 is suffering from high blood pressure. The bottom number (the second number mentioned) is the *diastolic* measurement. It is the pressure exerted when the heart is in the resting position between contractions. A diastolic rate of 90 is considered high. If the arteries are clogged or stiff, both numbers rise. The higher they rise, the harder your heart has to work. The harder your heart works, the sooner you succumb to heart disease.

Too much body fat, high sodium intake and smoking all adversely affect blood pressure—which can lead to heart disease, stroke or kidney problems. More and more doctors now prescribe exercise instead of medication for mildly high blood pressure. But your doctor must prescribe it, not you, me or anyone else.

Exercise lowers stress-related chemicals in the system and releases *endorphines,* which also reduce blood pressure. It increases HDL cholesterol (the good-guy cholesterol) that helps get rid of the LDLs (bad-guy cholesterol). Exercise lowers the resting heart rate and helps lower body fat to safer levels.

Exercise may not eliminate high blood pressure completely, but it definitely helps. As we've seen, you don't need vigorous workouts of 70 percent to 90 percent of your maximum heart rate, but rather moderate aerobics of perhaps 50 percent to 60 percent of your heart rate. You don't need to pump iron at the gym, which could be dangerous, but, rather, do gentle repetitions with very light weights.

Again, do not proceed without a doctor's advice.

Jet Lag

I used to walk off planes after even the shortest flights looking red eyed and pasty skinned—feeling fatigued, nauseated and headachey. I thought I was allergic to flying. Now I know my body was reacting to cigarette smoke, dehydration, lack of movement and slowed circulation.

Thankfully, we don't have to worry about smoke on U.S. flights anymore, and I now carry bottled water with me when I travel. I also carry fresh fruit and raw vegetables in a plastic container, and nibble on them throughout the flight. If a meal is served, I eat only what's healthy for me. I've also learned to exercise both before and after the flight. If the flight is long, there are exercises I can do *during* flight that help.

The rhythm of your nervous system can be disrupted by any flight, but especially those that are long enough to cross time lines. West-to-east travel is the most difficult, because of the time you lose. It can take a full day to recover for each time zone you cross. But you can combat that with exercise before, during and after the flight.

Here are some exercises anyone can do on an airplane, without disrupting others. Try them and see how much better you'll feel after your next flight:

1. While sitting down, bend from the waist and reach toward your feet. Try to hold the position for 20 to 30 seconds.
2. Roll your shoulders back 10 times. Then roll them forward 10 times.
3. Reach your hands above your head, clasp them together and stretch up, then side to side slightly—about an inch in either direction.
4. Lift one knee at a time and pull it to your chest with your hands. You should feel a stretch in the buttocks and thighs.
5. Flex one foot at a time—extending it as straight as possible and holding for 10 seconds. Repeat five times with each leg.
6. Do foot circles—five times each clockwise and counterclockwise.
7. Sit up straight, pull your stomach in tight, chest lifted, shoulders relaxed, press the palms of your hands together for five to ten seconds and release. Repeat the process five times.

After you arrive at your destination, do some aerobic exercise as soon as possible. Go for a brisk walk, jog or march in place in your room while you watch the news or use any available exercise equipment. I always take my own exercise tape or video with me and do it in my room, or make use of the stair-step machine, treadmill or exercise bike that many hotels now have.

Flight crews and athletes know that exercise works well to combat jet lag. We can learn from the experts. Exercise before, during and after travel will make you feel like a new person and get your system going right away. Eating right will enhance that. Don't put up with jetlag for even one more flight.

Fatigue

The most obvious solution to fatigue is to get more rest. Sometimes, however, we can't rest, are not sleeping well or don't feel rested even after we've slept. At those times, exercise and proper diet may be the solution.

Exercise increases your metabolism, helps you burn off toxins and enables you to sleep more soundly at night. It also improves your performance in the daytime. No matter what the reason for your fatigue, the right kind of exercise is sure to help. That is unless you are fatigued from over-exercising. In that case, get some rest.

If you are so fatigued that doing even the basic necessities for life is too exhausting for you, you need to know that you don't have to live that way. Exercising even for five to 10 minutes a day can make a difference in your energy level. It doesn't matter what you do—whether an aerobics class, a brisk walk, working on a stair-step machine, riding your exercise bike or doing isometric exercises at your desk—force yourself to get up and do something. The more you do, the less fatigued you will be.

Exercise creates a sense of well-being and optimism about life. A brisk walk can be the pick-up you need in the afternoon when sleepiness and fatigue set in. It will help you to get deeper, more rejuvenating sleep at night. It also helps you better digest, absorb and metabolize your food. At the same time, try going a couple of days eating only fresh vegetables and fruit. You'll find that if you force yourself to exercise and eat right, you'll have more energy and fatigue will become a thing of the past. If exercise doesn't alleviate your fatigue, see a doctor for a check up and get to the bottom of it.

You don't have to live with fatigue.

Premature Aging

Often, we view certain physical problems and limitations as inevitable, when in fact they could be prevented or minimized with regular exercise and more fruit, vegetables and whole grains.

Due to my genetic make-up, my body has never been very flexible, but about 15 years ago I found it becoming less and less flexible every year. When I could no longer touch my toes, lift the things I used to or walk up stairs without getting winded, I accepted it as part of the aging process. Then, I joined a health club to get in shape, and after three weeks of classes three times a week, I could do all of the above! I was amazed at so much improvement in so little time. And these were things I had accepted as inevitable.

How many physical limitations do *you* consider inevitable? How many conditions do you live with, not realizing that a little effort could free you of them? Too many, I suspect.

At any age or stage of our lives, we can improve cardiovascular endurance, muscular strength and flexibility, thereby slowing down the aging process. Stress ages us, but we can work against it with a good attitude, a healthy diet and proper exercise.

We tend to think our need for exercise diminishes as we get older. And we believe that disease and infirmity are inevitable, so we might as well live it up now before it comes. But there is much we can do to prevent the pain and disease we might experience otherwise.

Even if you have no interest in living to be 100, you probably don't want to be an invalid. I've found that many of the signs of aging, such as muscle weakness; brittle, shrinking bones; excess body fat and lack of endurance, are all due to sedentary lifestyles. Letting your muscles or cardiovascular system deteriorate reduces the amount of oxygen you can take into your system. Remember, the key to fat-burning and staying healthy is oxygen intake. You can be active into your 50s, 60s and 70s like you were in your 30s—if you stay consistent with an exercise program.

I've walked you through only a few of the

Stress ages us, but we can work against it with a good attitude, a healthy diet and proper exercise.

conditions that can be helped with proper exercise and healthy diet. I'm convinced that these two things, along with a good attitude, will benefit nearly anyone. I want you to be convinced too.

It's never too late to start an exercise program and improve your eating habits. Both are vitally important to a long, healthy, successful life, free of debilitating disease and infirmity. Be convinced enough to start your healthy program today. Remember, *prevention is the best medicine.*

Chapter 9

Powerful Tips For Busy Lives

You're busy. You're on the run. You've got family and friends to care for, a career to sustain, major responsibilities and commitments to fulfill. You don't have time to do in-depth research before making decisions about health and fitness. You don't even have a lot of time to spend on body-care activities.

If that's you, you may appreciate some short but powerful tips for making wise choices and integrating better body management into your life. If you were to firmly implant in your mind even *one* of these suggestions each day, your life would improve noticeably. Everything you do counts, so small steps add up to a big difference. Here goes:

Attitude Adjusters

- Unlike an old dog, you are *never* too old to change.
- Good posture starts in your mind. Think tall.
- If you don't *love* your work, find something that you *do* love. You'll live longer and be healthier.

- Remember, there are always two aspects to a situation: the way it really is, and the way we feel about it. Consider that the next time you start to get upset.
- Don't say you're on a diet. Say, "I'm committed to eating healthy."
- Whenever you eat, determine the reason and the emotions that accompany it. If it's for other than hunger and health, thoroughly examine the inner workings of your mind and emotions for hidden self-destruct buttons.
- There is a balance between being stressed-out and bored. Both can make you feel exhausted.
- Feeling depressed, bored, or blah? Then help someone else. It puts zest in your life, and nothing feels better than getting your mind off yourself.
- Be thankful for every bite of food you put into your mouth. It will aid digestion.
- It's easier to try and make small changes everyday, than to do a major change all at once.
- *Everyone* has enough time for two things—prayer and exercise. If you don't, you are too busy for your own good.
- It's okay to look good and feel healthy, so don't feel guilty about spending time and effort to get that way.
- Health is as much a matter of emotional well-being as it is physical fitness.
- Associate with people who are health conscious and work at staying fit. Their habits and choices will rub off on you.
- Long-term stress, depression or sadness breaks down the immune system.
- Think about being the best *you* can be, not about being someone you aren't or can never be.
- There is a strong connection between mind and body. Love and happiness have a positive effect; hate, fear and unforgiveness break down the immune system. Let this be a guide when you choose your daily responses to life.

Food for Thought

- Prepare simple recipes, using the freshest ingredients available.
- Store food in one-serving sizes, to avoid overeating and make it convenient to prepare.
- Whenever possible, cook extra to freeze and serve again.
- Get all who will eat a meal involved in preparing it. It keeps you from dropping from exhaustion, and gives everyone a chance to feel part of the event.
- When you eat meat, make it lean.
- The simpler the preparation, the healthier the food.
- Don't burn yourself on microwave food. Inside, it can be extremely hot, even though the outside feels cool.
- Have one less tablespoon of dressing on your salad. Cut down on butter or margarine—or don't use it at all.
- Reduce recipes by one egg and substitute two egg whites.
- Get used to using syrup and no butter on your low-fat, whole-grain waffles or pancakes.
- A tasty way to eat a baked potato is with equal parts of plain yogurt and cottage cheese mixed together and chopped green onions sprinkled on top.
- Use herbs and spices in place of salt.
- Eat *low-fat* or *non-fat* milk products.
- Avoid high sodium meals by doing your own cooking as much as possible.
- Invest in a vegetable steamer and steam your vegetables.

Get all

who will

eat a

meal

involved in

preparing

it.

Turkey tacos

can be

prepared the

same way as

beef tacos.

And they

taste great.

- Unless they have been frozen, try not to eat leftovers that are more than 24 hours old,
- If you don't like vegetables, try them stir-fried or mixed in with a pasta dish.
- Celebrate Thanksgiving more frequently, but on a smaller scale. Chicken, which is one of the leanest meats, is still 1-1/2 times fatter than turkey.
- For a healthful, guilt-free breakfast, pour fresh pureed strawberries on a homemade whole-wheat or rice and oat waffle, with a little honey if you wish. It's healthy, tasty and light.
- If you are using canned chicken broth, put it in the refrigerator beforehand and let the fat harden enough for you to scrape it off the top. Better yet, make your own stock and freeze it for future use.
- Fresh fruit is the best and quickest dessert. Serve it sliced, chopped, poached, baked, pureed or juiced.
- Here's my favorite way to prepare pasta: After it is drained, stir in a little olive oil, chopped-up fresh tomatoes and *fresh* basil. Top with a grated Romano cheese if you like. It's also good the next day cold, mixed with fresh raw vegetables and served as a pasta salad.
- Ground turkey is a good low-fat substitute for beef. Turkey tacos, for example, can be prepared the same way as beef tacos. And they taste great.
- If you don't like mushy oatmeal, buy whole-grain, unprocessed oats rather than the quick-cook kind. Bring the water to a boil, add the oats and let it cook for one minute. Then shut off the heat, cover with a lid and let it sit for about five minutes. It's great with a little honey and a chopped-up banana or strawberries on

it, if you don't want to use milk.

- Get used to lighter dressings. My favorite is a little olive oil with fresh lemon juice or balsamic vinegar. Add your favorite fresh herbs.
- For a great dressing, use different flavored vinegars like raspberry, balsamic, garlic and herb, along with a little olive oil.
- The more quickly you cook vegetables, the fewer vitamins will be destroyed in the process.
- Instead of frying, bake, broil, poach and steam.
- Substitute an equal amount of applesauce for oil or butter when you bake. It works well in cookies and cakes and changes the taste only slightly.

Out and About

- Fill up on fresh vegetable salad items *before* you eat anything else at a buffet or salad bar.
- If meals offered in a restaurant are too large, too fat or too unhealthy, try ordering side dishes. A baked potato, a salad and an order of asparagus makes a great lunch.
- Plan ahead what you will eat and where. You can always change your plans, but have a goal in mind.
- Order sandwiches with condiments on the side, so you know what and how much you are getting.
- Don't eat *anything* that has sugar in it.
- Not all food items at salad bars are good for you.
- Avoid all fried foods.
- Don't go to a restaurant unless you are sure they have something healthful to eat. Call ahead to find out.
- Ask for sauces and salad dressings on the side, then dip your fork in them before you pick up the food. You get the taste with less fat.
- Don't eat french fries. Instead, ask the server to substitute tomato slices, a vegetable or a baked potato.
- Blessed is he who finds an affordable restaurant that serves healthy, fresh food without salt, fat or sugar content.

No Laughing Matter?

If you aren't laughing much these days, it's time to get serious about finding humor in everyday events. Going to a funny movie, reading humorous literature or telling jokes is not enough. You need a lightness of heart (at the appropriate times, of course) that sees with a long-range perspective the humor in the mundane happenings of life. Your health is greatly affected by how much you laugh—and that's no laughing matter.

- If a serving in a restaurant is too large, eat only half of it and put the rest into a container to take home for lunch the next day. Another option is to ask the person you're eating with if they want to split a dinner.
- Salad bars are your best bet when eating out. But it usually costs two to three times more than preparing a salad at home from fresh produce you bought at the grocery store.
- Don't go to parties ravenous. Eat something healthful like a raw vegetable salad before you go, and imprint the words *low-fat, low-cal,* and *restraint* in red flashing lights in your brain. Keep in mind that this won't be the last time you'll ever eat for free.
- At parties, fill up on salads, vegetables and fruits and only *taste* the goodies.
- If you are having dinner at the home of a friend who thinks of corn chips as a vegetable, offer to bring the salad.
- At a party, drink sparkling water or fruit juice instead of high calorie, unhealthful drinks.
- When invited to dinner at a friend's home, tell him or her at the time you accept the invitation about any diet restrictions you have. Don't wait until you get there and find that the host or hostess has slaved all day making a wonderful

high-fat dinner with a high-fat dessert—just for you.

- If you must have fast food, get it from a salad bar. Most fast-food restaurants are installing them or serving ready made salads and low-fat meals. You can also eat only the meat out of a sandwich and remove the condiments or peel the skin off the chicken.
- Order the special low-fat meals offered in restaurants.

Exercise for Life

- Good athletic shoes are an investment in your future.
- Take ten minutes and do some physical activity with a child. (Toss a ball, walk around the block or jump rope.) It's not only good for *you*, but you'll have a lifelong friend.
- Over-exercising is the quickest way to end exercising altogether. Don't look for dramatic results overnight; instead, develop a lifestyle that promotes health for the long-term.
- Even 10 minutes of good aerobic exercise every other day is 100 percent better than no exercise at all.
- Older persons can improve their physical fitness at the same percentage rate as those who are much younger.
- Whenever it is safe to do so, use the stairs instead of taking the elevator.
- Don't drive around a parking lot looking for a parking place close to the front door. Park a little farther away (if it's safe) and enjoy the walk.
- Don't starve your body by severely restricting calories to lose weight—instead, exert more energy and burn calories through physical activity.
- When traveling, stay at hotels with exercise facilities. At home, using an exer-cycle in the laundry room is better than not getting any exercise at all.
- When doing *any* kind of physical activity, pay attention to breathing in and out, deeply and slowly.
- If you think you don't have time to exercise, try getting up 15 to 20 minutes earlier and ride an exer-cycle, work out to a 20

minute exercise video or march in place while you watch the morning news.

- Don't wait to get up earlier and exercise until you can go to bed early. If you first get up early and exercise, you *will* go to bed earlier that night.
- Decide in *advance* when you will exercise, and write it in your date book, like a doctor's appointment. If you do that often enough, you'll be writing it *instead* of a doctor's appointment.
- If at all possible, go for a walk after a meal. It helps digestion.
- Don't let a day go by without doing some form of stretching. Otherwise your body will become older than it has to be as you age.
- Take a walk instead of a snack.
- Every day, get down on your hands and knees and arch your back five times—like an angry cat. Your back and your posture are only as good as the muscles that keep them aligned.
- When beginning aerobic walking, walk only on flat surfaces. Once you are fit, you can go up and down hills.
- Walk with a friend—the conversation will be as invigorating as

Watching What You Eat

- Don't eat mindlessly, or do other things while you eat. Sit down, calmly pay attention to what you're eating and enjoy every bite.
- Don't eat unless you know you are eating out of hunger, or if it's been over four hours since your last meal.
- Don't eat food out of the box, bag, can or bottle it comes in. Put it on a plate so you will know how much you are eating.
- Don't skip meals. When you become hungry, you may forget restraint and overeat.

the walk.

- Vary your activities and the intensity of your workouts to avoid overuse and stress injuries.
- If you like to eat, be physically active so you burn more calories and can eat more food without weight gain.
- Avoid injury by always using exercise equipment that is in good condition.
- Walking jars the body and stimulates it to build bone mass.
- If your job is sedentary, take mini exercise breaks. Instead of snacking while on a break, stretch, walk or lift a small weight for 10 minutes.
- Rapid weight loss without exercise usually results in loss of muscle along with fat.
- Strong bones *now* will hold up better later on.
- Balance high-intensity activity or stress with periods of rest. If you don't, you can lose the ability to discern when you are overworking—until pain or sickness brings you to your senses.

Shop—Before You Drop

- When buying food, buy the freshest and best, not the cheapest. The best may also be the cheapest, but if it isn't, don't cut corners on your health.
- Spend most of your time in the grocery store on the outside aisles (produce department, meat and dairy sections) and move quickly through the center sections to pick up your whole-grain products. Those dangerous center aisles, where the highly-processed foods lurk, can be lethal to your health and your wallet.
- Avoid alcohol and drugs. Too much of either inhibits the liver's ability to detoxify the body.
- Don't bring food into the house that you know isn't healthy for you.
- Eat chicken without the skin and remember that white meat is lower in fat than dark meat.
- Fresh food is cheaper and tastier when it's in season.

- The more packaging and processing food undergoes, the more expensive it will be.
- Spend more in the produce department—and spend less on doctor bills, medicine, drugs and lost productivity.
- Vitamins cannot replace fresh vegetables.
- Do not grocery shop when you're hungry. Eat at least some fresh fruit before you go.
- Choose fresh foods over frozen foods and frozen foods over canned foods.
- For lowest fat content, choose water-packed tuna.
- Olive oil and canola oil are better for you.
- Grocery shop *after* you exercise. You'll feel less hungry and more like making healthy food choices.
- The word *enriched* on a label indicates that the natural nutrients in the food have been stripped out.
- Do "aerobics shopping." Put on your walking shoes when you go to the mall, and window shop at a fast pace.
- In the grocery store, leave your shopping cart in one place and walk to the shelves and back with your food items. (Unless they are too heavy to carry.)
- Buying the freshest, purest and highest quality foods means you don't have to do much preparation for them to taste great.
- Don't overlook cabbage-family vegetables. They help detoxify the body.
- When you bring fresh vegetables home from the market, immediately cut up some carrots, broccoli and cauliflower and shred some cabbage. Store them in plastic containers or zip-lock bags in the refrigerator. For a quick snack or meal, toss some together with a little olive oil and fresh lemon juice.

Healthy Habits

- A low-fat diet decreases the risk of cancer.
- It's not *how much* you eat, but *what* you eat that will make a difference. You don't have to go hungry in order to lose weight.
- If you finish eating a meal in less than twenty minutes, you're eating too fast.
- It's not what you take off, but what you *keep* off that counts.
- Include in your diet each week, at least one vegetable or fruit that you seldom eat. Variety is good for you and you may need the nutrients that particular food provides.
- Ask yourself if there is too much fat in the food *before* you eat it, not afterward.
- Companionship increases our sense of well-being, as well as improves our heart function and our ability to fight off disease.
- Try regular aerobics and fresh fruits and vegetables to reduce the effects of emotional stress.
- Have fish at least once a week, and buy it fresh.
- Learn to use the words *steamed, baked, poached, broiled, baked,* or *roasted* more often, and think of *fried* as a four letter word.
- Eat broth-based, rather than cream-based, soups.
- Eat food prepared without fat.
- Think of salad as more than head lettuce with a tomato slice. It can be any vegetable, raw or cooked, chopped and tossed together with a little dressing.

Carry

a bottle of

fresh pure

water

with you

wherever

you go.

And drink

from it

frequently.

- To keep your back straight while sitting, sit on the edge of your chair, put one foot out in front and the other one under the chair.
- Weigh yourself no more than once a month.
- Chew your food thoroughly. You'll absorb it better and avoid overeating.
- Simplify your eating habits. You don't need every nutrient every time you eat.
- A big, raw-vegetable salad should be a part of each day. Use low-fat dressing.
- Eat meatless meals at least ten times a week. That's less than half of the meals you'll have.
- If you are dying for something you shouldn't have, first fill up on a large, raw-vegetable salad and steamed vegetable—then go ahead and have that slice of pizza.
- Eat meals at regular times, at least four to five hours apart. If you must have a snack, eat only nutritious food.
- Get in the habit of carrying a bottle of fresh pure water with you wherever you go. And drink from it frequently.
- Eat plain yogurt and put *fresh* fruit in it rather than yogurt with fruit already added. You'll get more vitamins and fiber that way.
- Good eating and exercise habits start with good inner health habits.
- Your doctor's job is to cure you. It's *your* job to keep yourself healthy.
- Make fitness, worship and simple service to others a way of life.

Incredible Edibles

- A great vegetarian meal is tostadas. Take about 2 cups of pinto beans, rinse them and put them in a pan of water with about 4 inches over the top of the beans. Put 2 tomatoes, one onion and one garlic clove in a food processor and chop them finely, then add them to the pan of beans. Turn it on low and let it cook for five hours. When it's ready, strain the excess water off and add 1/4 cup grated jack cheese, stirring and mashing it into the beans. Serve over a tortilla that has been cooked crisp. On top of the beans put a layer of shredded lettuce, a layer of chopped tomatoes, guacamole and a sprinkle of shredded cheddar cheese. It's easy, fresh, tasty and *so* good for you.

- Make guacamole by adding one tablespoon of plain yogurt for every avocado. Then add the juice from one garlic clove and the juice from a tablespoon of chopped onions (run them through a garlic press). Put it all together in a food processor or mix it by hand.

- Use whole-wheat pita bread for a sandwich and fill it with a variety of raw, chopped vegetables topped with a healthful salad dressing. If you pack it in a lunch, put the vegetables and dressing in separate containers. Then, when you are ready to eat, mix them together and pour it all into your pita bread.

- To prepare quick and easy green beans, steam them until almost done. Then drain the water, put the beans in the empty pan along with a chopped onion, a little olive oil and some black pepper and stir it all together. Cover and let them set for five minutes while you prepare the rest of the meal. The taste of the onions will seep into the beans.

- When you have leftovers from dinner, consider tossing them together with a little olive oil and lemon or balsamic vinegar to make a great salad for lunch the next day. For a tasty, healthy salad, combine two or more of the following: corn *off* the cob,

145

green beans, boiled or baked potatoes, broccoli, squash, asparagus, green onions, green and red peppers, rice, bite-sized chicken or turkey pieces.

- For quick and easy carrots, put them in a pan with a cup or two of fresh-squeezed orange juice, and season with black pepper. Add a little butter, if your diet permits. Cook slowly over low heat about 30 minutes, or until done. Some people prefer them crisp, others like them soft.

Chapter 10

You Can Have Self-Control

My life once was out of control. I could eat nearly an entire cake by myself and drink alcohol until I couldn't stand up—all because I was unable to stop myself from doing something that felt good. There was so much pain, loneliness and rejection in my life that I grabbed at anyone and anything I thought could alleviate some of it, no matter what the consequences. Self-control to me was choosing marijuana over the equally available but far more scary and unpredictable LSD.

When everything in my life—health, career, emotions, relationships—hit rock-bottom, I was 28, although I looked and felt much older. In fact, even though I turned 50 this year, I don't feel nearly as old as I did back then. I felt that way because I did not know the right way to live—and I had zero self-control. I was miserable, undisciplined and chronically depressed. In my autobiography, *Stormie* (Harvest House, 1986), I told of my devastated life, and how I found complete restoration for my mind, body, soul, spirit and every part of my life. But I made one decision that changed my life forever—I read the Gospel of John in the Bible. As I did, I decided

Mini~Breaks Add Up

We often think vacations

have to be a minimum of at

least a weekend—or forget it.

It has to be the beach—or

no place at all. There are

advantages to an extended

time of rejuvenation, but

mini-breaks add up too.

Sometimes, taking a twenty-

minute walk after a meal,

eating lunch in a park or

driving to the lake to look at

the water for a half-hour can

make a huge difference in your

frame of mind. Even lying down

in a dark room for fifteen to

twenty minutes can make the

rest of your day better. These

mini-vacations can add up to a

longer, better quality of life.

to believe Jesus was who he said he was, and that he could do in my life what he said he would. In the Word of God, Jesus said that everything that happened in my life—past, present and future—would work out for good, as long as I looked to him to be the source of power to make it happen. If I looked to him in prayer, things that needed to happen, would happen.

A short time after that, I was counseled by a pastor's wife in preparation for God doing a mighty work of restoration from the results of a lifetime of wrong choices. When she suggested fasting, I winced. Having gone to bed hungry too often as a child, the thought of *deliberately* doing that for three days seemed out of the question. By that time, however, I had grown in the knowledge of God's ways enough to know that obedience to him would result in my greatest good.

"Lord, I want to do your will," I prayed, "but you know how undisciplined I am. If you want me to fast, you've got to help me."

I was amazed at how the Lord answered that prayer, sustaining and strengthening me through a difficult time. Not only did I receive freedom from fear and depression, but the experience became the first hard evidence of self-control blossoming in me. It grew from that first seed and spread to every part of my life. It amazed me how I became able to resist things I couldn't resist before, and became disciplined to do things I couldn't previously do.

Gradually, I learned that self-control is not just clenching your jaw and doing everything perfectly. It's a condition of the soul that begins in the heart *when there is an all-consuming desire to live God's way.* It has to do with saying, "Self, get out of the way—God is in control here." It's having the inner strength to stand and proclaim, as Jesus did, "For the glory set before me, I will do this."

That's what self-control is—inner strength. Inner strength is really *his* strength in us, enabling us to do what we cannot do on our own. If our inner strength is stronger than whatever tempts us, then we have self-control. If it isn't, we have no control.

Making New-Year's-type resolutions— "I will not drink," "I will not lie," "I will not gossip," "I will not overeat," "I will not look at pornography," "I will not be sexually immoral," "I will not overspend," "I will not give place to anger," or "I *will* exercise three times a week for the rest of my life"—dooms us to failure. On our own, our success rate in overriding our lusts is dismal. That's because strong-willed, self-determination produces rigidity, not *life.* Only the power of the Holy Spirit, working in harmony with our own will, can overcome the powerful lusts of our flesh.

When the Spirit is Willing, But . . .

In the Bible, we read about Peter who was so sure he would never deny knowing Jesus (Matthew 26:33-75). He was more than positive—he was *zealous.* He made up his mind, felt good about the decision—and that was that. No one wanted to do right more than Peter. Yet his flesh gave in to fear and he couldn't hold up to either his desire or his commitment.

Peter set himself up for failure because although his spirit was willing, his flesh was weak. He trusted in his flesh instead of trusting God to strengthen him in his spirit and to give him divine enablement. Jesus said, "Watch and pray, lest you enter into temptation. The *spirit* is indeed willing, but the *flesh* is weak" (Matthew 26:41).

Have you ever found that just when you've committed to do something, it becomes nearly impossible? I can think of a number of times that has happened to me. For example, 20 years ago I began a habit of praying early in the morning, because I wanted to get closer to God and to experience the peace of his presence. Since then, I can remember three times when I had problems spending time with God. On all three occasions I had made a specific commitment to do it . . .

The first time, a visiting pastor teaching at our church asked us to commit to spending an hour in prayer every day. The second time was at a seminar on prayer, that emphasized making a specific time-commitment each day to pray. The third time, I heard an author of a book on prayer talking on the radio about spending an hour with God daily. On each occasion, the moment I committed to spend a certain amount of time in prayer faithfully each day, it became nearly impossible to do so. Even the time I had previously been spending in prayer was stolen from me. Before, an hour in prayer had seemed too short and I'd felt I could spend all day in God's presence. Suddenly, finding and spending *any* amount of time seemed difficult.

Were those people wrong to teach us to commit to one hour of prayer a day? No, I don't believe so. I believe the problem was in my making the commitment to do it *in the flesh*—which is weak. It has to be a spiritual commitment. The ground-work has to be laid in prayer. I had to be led by the Lord to do it, and I had to acknowledge that it couldn't happen without the Holy Spirit's power enabling me.

Instead of merely determining to do it, I should have said: "Lord, I want to spend an hour a day with you. Help me to do that. Help me to clear a space in my schedule. Call me when it's time. Make the desire in my heart for more of your presence so strong that I long to spend time with you above all other things I could be doing."

When I *did* pray that prayer, I couldn't wait to spend time with God. And the more I did, the more I wanted to do so.

Every time I commit to something—writing a book, an article, a song, or doing an exercise video—I first ask the Lord if I should do it. That way I am confident that I have the go-ahead from him.

Immediately after I agree to doing it, I am struck with the impossibility of it ever coming to pass. I know that on my own I don't have the ability, strength, time or knowledge I need to do the job the way I think it should be done. The sense of being unable to fulfill my commitment is overwhelming. This happens *every* time! When it does, I immediately get before the Lord. My sense of being overwhelmed actually propels me to my knees, and I say, "Lord, I know you've called me to do this—but I can't do it on my own. I especially can't do it the way I know it should be done. Lord, I depend on you to do it through me. Give me *your* wisdom and strength."

I also experience the same thing with regard to exercising regularly and eating properly. When I try to do either of them in my own strength, I eventually fail. I overeat more than ever, and I can't seem to find the time to exercise. I make the commitment, but there is always something keeping me from my goal. But when I surrender my whole self, body and all, to the Lord, I see results. I say, "God, *you* be in charge of my health. *You* show me how much I should exercise. *You* show me what and how much I should eat. I depend on you, because by myself I can do nothing. With you, all things are possible. Lord, show me what to do, how to accomplish it, and enable me to do it."

Changing lifelong habits can only be accomplished by first giving the burden to God, then totally depending on him every day. We can accomplish nothing lasting ourselves—so don't set yourself up for failure by trying to do it in the flesh.

Changing lifelong habits can only be accomplished by first giving the burden to God, then totally depending on him every day.

Make this exchange a step at a time, day by day. Pray: "Lord, help me today to live your way, think your way, act your way, work your way and talk your way."

Don't worry about whether you're going to be able to do it tomorrow. Tomorrow you'll seek God again and ask for a fresh *flow* of his Spirit of love, strength, wisdom and enablement. *Put God in charge today.*

Making Changes That Last

I know you wouldn't have read this far if you didn't want to make changes that are permanent. The only way for that to happen with any degree of significance is to first completely surrender yourself and your life to God—and then to love him more than you love anything else.

Our world suffers from a deficiency of self-control because we'd rather be lovers of fleshly lusts than lovers of God. Too often, we entertain the darkness that lurks in our hearts rather than fleeing from it. We give place to a secret life that we deceive ourselves into thinking that God doesn't see. We sometimes act as if being controlled by the flesh is without consequences. We don't see that what we do not only produces death in *us*, but it affects *everyone* around us, even if we do it completely in secret. We mistakenly think we're exercising our freedom as we indulge our flesh, when in fact we're becoming enslaved to it. We think we're happier doing whatever we want, but the truth is we're happier when we choose to restrain ourselves.

The only way to gain the inner strength of self-control is to surrender completely to God in humble prayer, praise and worship—then to show our love for him through obedience. Only then can we become God-controlled. Only then can we become empowered by his Spirit to make right decisions. Only then can we make changes that last.

Better body management begins in the heart.

Once we determine to be lovers of God and his way, we can take steps to avoid setting ourselves up for failure in areas where we are weak. If our weakness is sexual immorality, we don't have lunch alone with an attractive person of the opposite sex. If our problem is alcohol, we don't go to places that serve it or sell it. If our problem is gossiping, we don't talk with people who love to hear it. If overeating is our downfall, we don't bring enticing food into our home, nor do we go places where we can easily get it. Instead, we continually ask the Holy Spirit for divine strength to walk away from whatever tempts us. We aren't just innocent victims of our lusts; we're responsible for aiming ourselves in the right direction. We're responsible for asking the Holy Spirit to plant the seeds that grow the inner strength to make right decisions. We're also responsible for preparing our hearts to nurture those seeds. The wholeness and successful, long, healthy life we all desire will elude us if we don't.

Before I came to know the Lord, I couldn't control any part of my life. I still can't. Only now I'm convinced that I can't, but *God* can. God helps me to "discipline my body and bring it into subjection" (1 Corinthians 9:27, NKJV), and to "make no provision for the flesh, to fulfill its lusts" (Romans 13:14).

God helps me avoid compromising situations, tell the truth when it would be easier to lie, not repeat juicy tidbits of information, not say what I'm thinking when someone is rude, not eat junk when I have an abundance of it at my fingertips, not find a million other things to do when I need to spend time in prayer, not sit and watch T.V. when I need to give my body exercise.

Recently, our entire church finished a three-day fast, and it was no easier for me this time than it was 20 years ago. But God sustained me and gave me the inner strength to control my desire to eat. I didn't keep from eating because I was self-controlled, but because I was *God*-controlled.

Do I do things perfectly all the time? Not at all. But when I get out-of-hand in the eating and exercise departments, I go back to my Source of power to make things right. I ask the Lord for his help, because I know what I'm made of and how little I can do on my own.

You may struggle with controlling your diet and exercise, as many people do. But I encourage you to find your motivation internally rather than externally. External motivation will *never* consistently sustain you. Trying to lose 50 pounds by the high-school reunion, trying to fit into the little red dress by Christmas, trying to wear your bathing suit by summer or trying to be attractive to a certain person will never be enough motivation to make the lifestyle changes you desire.

You need the power that penetrates the deepest level of your being—God's power.

Born With a Purpose

In case no one has ever told you this, I close with God's truth about you. Read this every day for a year, if you have to, to make it part of who you are:

The truth is, you are a unique and special creation of God. You weren't an accident, no matter what you've been led to believe. Even if your mother or father were surprised by you, God wasn't. God knows the plans he has for you, and they are for good and not for evil. They are plans to give you a future and a hope. He has a high purpose for your life and what happens to you matters to him. He wants what matters to him to matter to you. He says you need never be discouraged about yourself or your life, no matter how hopeless things may seem, because *with him all things are possible.* No matter what your age, your life is just beginning. You can make a fresh start today. You never have to be limited by your past, because God sees you through your future.

He wants you to see yourself that way too.

"It is not good to be preoccupied with your body but it is wise to value the temple God has given you!"
Stormie Omartian

$19.98 Sugg. Retail
VHS Video

Stormie Omartian's new 45-minute, low impact aerobic workout video is specifically designed to help burn fat and strengthen the cardiovascular system. Includes 6 minutes of warm-up, 28 minutes of moderate intensity, 5 minutes of cool-down, plus 6 minutes of muscle toning for the abdominal, inner thigh and buttock areas.